JACQUELINE KENNEDY ONASSIS

JACQUELINE
KENNEDY
ONASSIS

Ellen Ladowsky

A Balliett & Fitzgerald Book

PARK LANE

NEW YORK

To Nana—E.L.

This 1997 edition is published by Park Lane Press,
a division of Random House Value Publishing, Inc.,
a Random House Company
201 East 50th Street, New York, New York 10022

A&E's acclaimed BIOGRAPHY series is available on videocassette from
A&E Home Video. Call 1-800-423-1212 to order.

A&E and **BIOGRAPHY** are trademarks of A&E Television Networks,
registered in the United States and other countries.

Park Lane Press and colophon are trademarks of
Random House Value Publishing, Inc.

Random House
New York • Toronto • London • Sydney • Auckland
http://www.randomhouse.com/

Printed and bound in the United States of America

A Balliett & Fitzgerald Book
Series Editor: Thomas Dyja
Book Design: Lisa Govan, Susan Canavan
Photo Research: Maria Fernandez
Copy Editor: William Drennan
and special thanks to Judy Capadanno, Bill Huelster,
and John Groton at Random House

Library of Congress Cataloging-in-Publication Data

Ladowsky, Ellen, 1964-
  Jacqueline Kennedy Onassis : Biography / Ellen Ladowsky
        p.   cm.   —(Biographies from A&E)
    Includes bibliographical references.
      1. Onassis, Jacqueline Kennedy, 1929–1994. 2. Celebrities—
United States—Biography. 3. Presidents' spouses—United States
—Biography. I. Title. II. Series.
CT275.0552L33 1997
973.922'092—dc20
(B)   96-36064
                                                            CIP

ISBN 0-517-20077-5
10 9 8 7 6 5 4 3 2 1
First Edition

CONTENTS

circa 1945

CHAPTER ONE

CHILDHOOD

When the announcement was made in the spring of 1928 that John "Jack" Bouvier III would wed Janet Lee, much of New York society was skeptical: Jack, a handsome, charismatic thirty-eight-year-old stockbroker, had reneged on two previous engagements. Tall and dark, with a pencil-thin mustache and wide-set blue eyes, he was often mistaken for Clark Gable and had a list of vices as long as Rhett Butler's. His roguish behavior and his reputation as a chronic gambler, a heavy drinker, and a notorious womanizer all earned him the nickname "Black Jack."

His fiancée could hardly have been more different. Sixteen years his junior and an accomplished equestrienne, the fashionable Janet Lee was schooled in the virtues of discipline and propriety. Where Black Jack was warmhearted, spontaneous, and rakish, she was chilly, reserved, and genteel. And while he mocked the conventions of polite society, she was an aggressive social climber who clung to Establishment rules and rituals. They did, however, share one interest: Both were eager to make—and spend—money.

Although both families were decidedly upper crust, the Bouviers held themselves to be above the Lees. An established Catholic clan, the Bouviers had come into their wealth and position several generations earlier; by comparison, the Lees seemed nouveau riche. Janet's father, James Lee, had made his own millions financing real-estate estate deals, wealth he then skillfully used to obtain entry into society. In time he became vice president of Chase National Bank and then president of New York Central Savings Bank. The Lees, for their part, entertained some disdain for the old-line Bouviers—and they were not alone. As someone close to the family explains, there was a general feeling among New York's elite that "the seed had gone to rot."

Not surprisingly, then, Janet's father strongly disapproved of the match. As a businessman, James Lee took a dim view of Jack's spendthrift ways, crushing debts, and playboy habits. But he decided not to oppose the engagement. Interference, he felt, might hasten the marriage, whereas if they met no opposition, the young couple might soon tire of each other and break up. Much to her father's displeasure, and to the surprise of many others, the ceremony was performed on July 7, 1928, at St. Philomena's Church in East Hampton, Long Island, before five hundred guests. It was a society event: lavish and traditional.

James Lee's suspicions about his son-in-law quickly proved justified. Jack began misbehaving even before the honeymoon with Janet was over. While they were sailing to England on the *Aquitania*, he absented himself from his new bride to spend time with young tobacco heiress Doris Duke. After only a year, the marriage was foundering. Yet there was hope that the impending birth of their first child would settle him down. On July 28, 1929, during a weekend visit to the Hamptons, Janet gave birth to a baby girl—who arrived six weeks late. Named after her father, Jacqueline Lee Bouvier weighed eight pounds and, like her father, had dark hair and wide-set eyes. Her parents immediately started calling her Jackie.

But the year of Jackie's birth proved to be an especially difficult one for Jack Bouvier. In October 1929, Jack's only brother, Bud, died of cirrhosis of the liver. Jack was devastated by the loss, and while he was still grieving, the stock market crashed on October 24. Up to that point, Jack had been earning enough to support his profligate habits. After the crash, however, the Bouviers had two choices: scale back their lifestyle or go cap in hand to their families. Black Jack chose the latter. While Jack's father underwrote the summer home they rented in East Hampton, James Lee allowed his daughter and her husband to live in an eleven-room apartment on Park Avenue that he owned and loaned them money from time to time. The loan from Janet's father was interest-free, but it did not come without strings. Janet's father demanded that Black Jack curtail some of his more expensive acquisitions and account for his earnings and expenses. Jack was humiliated and resentful. His spending spun out of control and he began to drink even more heavily. On November 27, 1931, a second stock market crash, known as Black Friday, set him back even further.

Despite these financial problems, little Jackie had a privileged upbringing, complete with nannies, private schools, riding lessons, and Hamptons vacations. She was always beautifully dressed and groomed, and her playroom was replete with toys from the best Manhattan stores. Jackie was first written up in the newspaper when she was only two years old. A

Janet Lee with daughter Jackie, circa 1932.

local East Hampton paper sent a society columnist to her second birthday party. Behind the facade of carefree wealth, however, Jack and Janet were arguing almost constantly about
money. Yet despite their marital discord, the couple had
another baby when Jackie was three and a half years
old—Caroline Lee, whom the family called Lee. She was a

soft, sweet-natured, cuddly little child who was very attached to her mother—Jackie on the other hand was independent and strong-willed. "She [Jackie] was of tougher intellectual fiber," one family member observed. One of the often told family childhood stories about Jackie illustrates her remarkable self-possession and fierce independence. When Jackie was four years old, her nanny took her and Lee on a walk in Central Park. Jackie promptly wandered off and got lost. She was eventually approached by a concerned police officer, who asked the young child why she was alone. Jackie was not crying or frightened. She coolly replied that her nurse and baby sister seemed to be lost.

According to her mother, Jackie was a steady reader. She also showed an early talent for sketching and enjoyed writing poetry about nature or animals, a hobby encouraged by her paternal grandfather, who often wrote verses for his grandchildren. She was also inordinately attached to a tattered rag doll named Sammy that she played with for endless hours.

Although as an adult Jackie was perceived to be too lady-like for the Kennedy touch football games, as a child she had a distinct tomboyish streak. Her mother put her on a horse for the first time at age one. By the time Jackie was five, she was entering horse shows. The Bouviers kept seven horses at the East Hampton riding club, and Jackie's mother eventually gave her one as a gift, a brown mare named Danseuse.

If Jackie was trying to win her equestrienne mother's approval, one anecdote indicates that it was not easily given. In a jumping competition at the Southampton Horse Show, Jackie approached one of the fences at the wrong angle. Frightened, the pony stopped short, throwing her to the ground. She immediately picked herself up and attempted to get back in the saddle. But she was confused and tried to mount on the wrong side, causing the amused audience to clap and cheer. In the car on the way home, Jackie asked her mother why the audience had clapped when she fell off. "They didn't know what really happened," Janet scolded her six-year-old daughter. "You should be ashamed of handling your pony so carelessly. He might have been hurt."

Janet seemed to prefer Lee. When Jamie Auchincloss, Jackie's half brother, recently thumbed through an old family album from the thirties and early forties, he was arrested by the captions Janet had written under two photographs of the girls. "There was a picture of Jackie," Auchincloss recalls, "and it just said, 'Jackie,' and on the next page there was a picture of Lee, and underneath it it said, 'My Lee.' "

Jackie identified with her father, and by the time she entered kindergarten was displaying his appetite for mischief. At Miss Chapin's, an exclusive New York private elementary school, she was very popular with her classmates but earned a reputation as an unrepentant troublemaker. Not one for drab conformity, Jackie hated to wear the school's traditional blue linen uniform. Her teachers considered her a "problem child" claiming she was very bright but disruptive and unruly. With great regularity, Jackie was dispatched to the office of the headmistress, Miss Ethel Stringfellow, for engaging in what today would be considered very un-Jackie-like behavior. "Jackie was acting up and doing some wonderfully funny but scatological tricks on her teachers, putting cold cream on the toilet bowls," reports Jamie Auchincloss. Miss Stringfellow finally devised a creative way of explaining to Jackie why she needed to be better behaved. Knowing how much she loved riding, the headmistress told her to think of herself as a horse. "I know you love horses and you yourself are very much like a beautiful Thoroughbred," she told the young girl. "But if you're not properly broken and

Black Jack Bouvier leads his daughter Jackie on her pony.

trained, you'll be good for nothing." The teacher's words made a strong impression on the young girl.

It's unclear how much of Jackie's acting-up could be attributed to the disintegration of her parents' marriage. It seems likely she would have overheard their bitter, late-night arguments and probably would have known about her father's womanizing and gambling. She definitely knew about his drinking. According to biographer Ed Klein, Jackie frequently observed her father hitting her mother. She also saw him lying on the living room couch in a drunken stupor. "Before he passed out," Klein wrote in *All Too Human*, "Jackie and her mother would carry him to the bedroom, undress him, and clean up his vomit and urine. The next morning she would witness his tearful apologies as he begged his wife and daughters to forgive him and pleaded for one more chance." But those who knew Jackie well as a child say it was almost impossible to tell how much she felt about her parents marital dissension. She had already perfected a technique of hiding her emotions, another trait she would exhibit throughout her life.

It was very clear, however, whose side she took in her parents' disputes. Although she shared many of her mother's interests, Jackie adored her high-spirited father, who doted on her endlessly. She felt that her father, not her mother, was the real victim in the marriage. This childhood attachment resembles that of another former First Lady, Eleanor Roosevelt, whose father, Elliot, an irresponsible but charming alcoholic, could do no wrong in his daughter's eyes. As with Eleanor, this skewed interpretation of reality would have a profound influence on Jackie's adult choices, particularly her romantic ones.

⬧ ⬧ ⬧

"Ambition: Not to be a housewife."

A telling photo from the summer of 1934 sums up how desperate the Bouviers' marital situation had become. In the photo, Jackie's father and an attractive young woman are holding hands, while Janet stands by, seemingly unaware. When the picture was published in the *New York Daily News*, Janet was furious. She had been prepared to overlook Jack's liaisons as long as they remained private, but she would not tolerate public embarrassment.

On September 30, 1936, she initiated a six-month trial separation. Jack moved into the Westbury Hotel and visited the children on weekends, taking them on outings to the movies, the zoo, the museum, and showering them with gifts and treats. Once he took them to the Stock Exchange, where he proudly paraded the girls out on one of the balconies to the delighted applause of the crowd below. Jackie and Lee, in turn, began hamming it up, curtsying like princesses.

Jackie loved her father's visits and became much more cheerful when she was around him. Where her mother emphasized appropriate behavior and an almost Victorian code of reserve, he encouraged Jackie to be assertive. As she grew older, Jackie's own public persona would somehow reconcile these seemingly opposite directives. She learned to stand out by being guarded; she perfected an image of flamboyant correctness.

When the six-month separation was up, the Bouviers got back together at Jack's suggestion. Black Jack's behavior, however, did not change, and the constant quarreling quickly resumed. By the end of September the couple had once again separated. Jack didn't want to lose his daughters and appealed to Janet's father to use his influence to sway her. But by this point James Lee despised Black Jack and was actively encouraging his daughter to seek a divorce.

She took his advice. Janet and the girls moved from their spacious Park Avenue living quarters into a smaller apartment, at One Gracie Square. Nannies caring for Jackie at the time report that Janet, who was under great duress, drank heavily and disciplined the children often far out of proportion to the offense. During this unstable period, nine-year-old Jackie's personality changed dramatically. According to friends and family members, the once-boisterous little girl became shy and distant.

By mid-1939 Janet was in the throes of divorce proceedings.

She retained a lawyer, who advised her to hire a private detective to conduct surveillance on her husband in order to obtain proof of adultery. The investigator had no difficulty uncovering the evidence, which he then leaked to the press. On January 26, 1940, the *New York Daily Mirror* printed an article in the society pages with the headline: "SOCIETY BROKER SUED FOR DIVORCE." Furious, Black Jack had his lawyer attempt to gather damaging information on Janet. When Janet's lawyer learned of this, he advised her to go to Nevada, where divorces were easier to obtain. Janet spirited the children to a Reno hotel for a vacation, where they swam and rode until she met the six-week resident requirement. The divorce hearing took place on July 22, 1940. It lasted less than twenty minutes. Jackie's father sent a lawyer but did not attend.

The battle between Jack and Janet then shifted to a tug-of-war for the children's affections. Jackie's father plied her with expensive gifts. Her mother made it clear that she viewed her ex-husband as an irresponsible cad, not least by implicitly comparing him to her new love interest, Hugh Auchincloss.

Auchincloss was eminently respectable and very eligible; when he and Janet met, he was a founding partner in an investment banking firm. He had previously worked as a lawyer in New York City, and had served in the federal government. Of Scottish descent, the Auchincloss family were old-stock upper class and, unlike the Bouvier family, staid and proper. "The word 'swashbuckling' has never been applied to an Auchincloss, as far as I know," says Hugh's son Jamie Auchincloss. "The whole Auchincloss family marked itself down as having golf as its sport, being Presbyterian and conservative and Republican, going to Yale, and living in New York City and working in the Stock Exchange, all things that were very accepted and not very adventurous."

✦ FAMILY TREE ✦

Both the Bouvier family and the Lee family were well-to-do. Janet's father, James Lee, was a self-made millionaire. He made his fortune in real estate and went on to become the vice president of Chase National Bank and then president of New York Central Savings Bank. The Bouvier family had obtained wealth and status in society several generations before the Lees and consequently considered themselves to be higher on the social ladder. Jackie's grandfather had been in the *Social Register* since its inception, yet the Bouviers were not truly part of what was thought of as high society.

As Bouvier cousin John Davis writes in *The Bouviers*, "the second generation of Bouviers were the affluent children of a nouveau riche immigrant from southern France who happened to marry well and have his children marry even better. As such they occupied a layer of American society that was respectable, polite, reticently fashionable, and 'comfortably well off,' but was not Society with a capital S."

One thing the two families did have in common was the readiness to lie about their roots, a habit that was not uncommon around the turn of the century. Jackie's grandfather, John Vernou Bouvier, Jr., wrote and privately published a book of bogus Bouvier genealogy that claimed that the Bouviers had descended from noble lineage. Titled *Our Forebears*, it was dedicated to his grandchildren, and it traced the Bouvier family back to French aristocracy. In reality the Bouviers were descendants of petite bourgeoisie.

The Lees also enhanced their family background. Jackie's mother, Janet, boasted that they they were related to Robert E. Lee. Jackie's half brother, Jamie Auchincloss, who once worked in the National Archives, says he has never been able to trace his mother's side of the family beyond her grandfather. "It was a very incomplete family genealogy," says Auchincloss, "and I figured in one way or another it was incomplete because something had been made up to make them more socially respectable in the New World."

In his autobiography, *Palimpsest*, Gore Vidal suggests that Jackie's maternal grandfather was Jewish and "had changed his name in order to become the first Jew to be a vice president of the Morgan bank." But Jamie Auchincloss says that Vidal's assertion has never been proven. "That was one of the things that I think people said to be either funny or nasty, depending on one's point of view."

While the entire Auchincloss clan was well-off, Hugh Auchincloss was particularly wealthy. His maternal grandfather had been a partner of John D. Rockefeller in Standard Oil. Auchincloss owned two homes—one on the Virginia shore, another near Narragansett Bay in Newport—belonged to the toniest clubs, and mingled with all the "right" people. From Hugh Auchincloss's two previous marriages, he was well acquainted with the role of stepfather. One of his stepchildren was author Gore Vidal. He also had three children of his own from his earlier marriages, all of whom lived with him: Yusha from his first wife, and Nina ("Nini") and Thomas from his second.

In the spring of 1942, Janet and Auchincloss married and the children moved with their mother into the Auchincloss residence in Virginia. Jackie and Lee were heartbroken to be taken so far away from their father, but the luxury of their new surroundings helped soften the blow. Merrywood, the Auchincloss winter residence, was an enormous Georgian-style brick mansion in McLean, Virginia, with forty-six acres of steep, wooded hills with lots of brambles. There was an Olympic-size swimming pool, an indoor badminton court, stables, and riding trails. Their summer home in Newport, Hammersmith Farm, was a sprawling twenty-eight-room estate set on eighty-three acres. Janet, for her part, was thrilled to have married Hugh. Unlike her first husband, he was a very stable and gentle man as well as a loyal husband.

Jackie and Lee were also fond of their new stepfather, who they called "Uncle Hughdie," conflating his first name and middle initial. Nevertheless, he suffered in comparison to their charismatic father. According to one popular story, he took all the frozen food out of his freezer in the winter and moved it to the porch so he could save money by turning off the deep freeze. And unlike the magnetic Black Jack, a compelling

The Auchincloss/Bouvier family pose for a Christmas card photo.
From the top: Jackie, Yusha, Nina, Lee, Thomas, Janet, baby Janet,
and Hugh, 1945.

raconteur, Auchincloss was considered to be something of a
dullard who told the same stories over and over again. However,
he is reported to have had one eccentric hobby that complicates

this impression: He compiled an extensive collection of pornography.

The more Jackie grew to accept her new life, the more unhappy Black Jack became. He was furious at Janet, and felt his daughters had abandoned him. His drinking became so uncontrolled that he eventually checked himself into an alcohol rehabilitation center. He never remarried. His most serious relationship was with a British officer's wife, who was present one summer when the children came to visit. Eventually, however, she and her husband returned to England. Jackie's father later received a letter from the woman saying that she had delivered twins—a boy and a girl—and Black Jack was the father.

In 1944, after two years of study at Holton Arms, Jackie was sent away to Miss Porter's, an exclusive all-girls boarding school in Farmington, Connecticut. It was here among the girls from the best families in New York that Jackie mastered high society behavior. Jackie roomed with an old friend from Miss Chapin's, Nancy Tuckerman ("Tucky," as she was known back then). Over the next few years the two girls became inseparable.

At Miss Porter's Jackie was considered a good student, earning an A-minus average. She never dated and was shy and a bit of a loner, according to schoolmates. "I just know no one will ever marry me and I'll end up as a housemother at Farmington," she told a friend. But those who did get to know her well say she had an offbeat sense of humor. Her favorite extracurricular activity was drama. She joined "The Farmington Players," the school's theatre group. She had already developed her own highly individual style, never wearing the traditional skirts and sweaters favored by her contemporaries, opting instead for less conservative, more dramatic clothing.

Jackie's father frequently made the trip from New York to the nearby Connecticut boarding school. While visiting, Black

Jack often spoke to his teenage daughter in indelicate ways, recounting his sexual exploits. According to Klein, Jackie and her father played a game where Jackie would point to the mothers of the girls at her school and ask which one he had slept with. "That one, Daddy?" she would ask. "Oh yes," he would say, "I've already had her." He told his daughter how he had cheated on her mother while they were still on their honeymoon, which Jackie apparently found funny and relayed to her classmates.

Much as she enjoyed them, visits with her father made her feel anxious. Although Black Jack never told her about his financial problems, it was clear to Jackie that his situation had grown far worse. Jackie already felt poor amid the opulence of her friends' lives. It was the custom for girls at Miss Porter's to board their own horses. When Jackie's parents wouldn't give her the necessary money, she appealed to her grandfather. She wrote him a letter that included pointed remarks about her "deprivation" and sent him some poems she had written for him. He sent the money right away. With her circumstances improved, she fired off another letter to her mother saying that her horse Danseuse was reduced to "wearing a stolen blanket which I snitched from another horse." Embarrassed, her mother sent the money. Scheming like this perhaps led her classmates to nickname her "Jacqueline Borgia."

Jackie hadn't entirely lost the rebellious streak she had displayed at Miss Chapin's. She often broke school rules, smoking in her dorm and stealing late-night snacks from the school kitchen. Once she dumped a pie in an unpopular teacher's lap. Yet her most renowned act of defiance at Miss Porter's occurred when Jackie posed for a classmate's camera with her schoolgirl sweater pulled down low over her shoulder, her hair tousled in front of her face, and her lips in a sex-

Jackie smoking, circa 1945.

kittenish pout. One of the photographs found its way to the office of the headmaster, who was shocked and immediately notified her mother.

While Jackie was away at school, her mother had two children with Hugh Auchincloss: Janet, Jr., born in 1945, and

Jamie, born in 1947, right before Jackie returned home. When Jackie graduated from Miss Porter's School at seventeen, her entry in the yearbook read as follows:

Favorite song: "Lime House Blues"

Always saying: "Play a Rhumba."

Next most known for: Wit

Aversion: People who ask if her horse is still alive

Where found: Laughing with Tucky

There was also one more line, which read, "Ambition: Not to be a housewife."

Newport, 1947

CHAPTER TWO

DEBUTANTE

In the summer of 1947, though it was already thought of as charmingly old-fashioned, and was by no means considered mandatory, it remained the custom for a young upper-class woman to make a formal entrance into the social world around the time of her eighteenth birthday. "Coming out" served as an announcement to the public that the girl was of an age to be courted. It was also a test of her social talents. Jackie herself made the decision to participate in this ritual.

Instead of a debut at one of the large cotillions in New York, Jackie's mother hosted an afternoon tea dance that June for three hundred guests at Hammersmith Farm, the Auchincloss Newport estate. The reception was given largely for her parents' friends. Held on the same day as the christening of Jackie's new half brother, the guests were invited "To meet Miss Jacqueline Lee Bouvier and Master James Lee Auchincloss." "Many women of Newport brought their eligible daughters to meet me, not realizing I was six months old," says Jamie Auchincloss.

A few weeks later in July, a joint coming-out party was thrown at Newport's Clambake Club in honor of Jackie and Rose Grosvenor, the daughter of one of Hugh Auchincloss's friends. The formal dinner-dance, cohosted by the Auchincloss and Grosvenor families, was mainly for the teenage friends of the two girls. Jackie wore white—the preferred color for debutantes—to both parties. Her mother had been ill on the day Jackie went shopping and was apparently disappointed with the dress she had picked out for the dinner-dance. She had wanted her daughter to wear an expensive designer gown like the Dior original that Rose wore, but instead Jackie had bought a simple off-the-rack dress that cost less than $60. Still, she won rave reviews. One society page column hailed it as "a lovely white tulle gown with an off-the-shoulder neckline and bouffant skirt."

Lee Bouvier ensured that her older sister Jackie didn't monopolize the spotlight. Lee had been given permission to attend the party after dinner, but rather than wearing the tasteful dress her mother had chosen for her, the curvaceous fourteen-year-old turned up in a sexy, strapless pink satin gown with long black satin fingerless gloves. The dress had the desired effect: Jackie's male friends flocked around Lee all evening. Janet was horrified at the sight of her younger daughter in such a vampish outfit, particularly in the company of Jackie's very proper friends. Jackie was shocked, too, but as the evening went on, she decided her sister's fashion rebellion was more funny than mortifying. She and Lee good-humoredly named the gown the "siren suit," and Jackie later borrowed it herself.

For the rest of the year, Jackie made the rounds of debutante balls in New York, Long Island, and Newport, an early exposure that brought her the highest possible honor: Igor Cassini, who was then writing the "Cholly Knickerbocker" society column, declared Jackie "Debutante of the Year." His top-drawer gossip column appeared in the *New York Journal-American* and was syndicated in hundreds of papers around the country, putting her in the nation's eye at age eighteen.

"America is a country of traditions," Cassini wrote. "Every

Debutante of the Year with fellow deb Rose Grosvenor.

four years we elect a president, every two years our congressmen. And every year, a new Queen of Debutantes is crowned. . . . The Queen Deb of the year for 1947 is Jacqueline Bouvier, a regal brunette who has classic features and the daintiness of Dresden porcelain."

Cassini, who had met her only briefly during the social season, later recalled that it was atypical for him to have selected Jackie as Queen Deb: "I usually tried to choose one of the prettier, flashier society girls," he explained. ". . .Yet I felt something very special in her, an understated elegance. . . . Although shy and extremely private, she stood out in a crowd. She had that certain something."

❱ ❱ ❱

"Hold your meter, driver."

Being named Debutante of the Year was an unusual distinction for Jackie, who had never before been singled out for her beauty. In fact, although naturally attractive, Jackie didn't go out of her way to play up her looks at that point in her life. At five-seven, she had an equestrienne's figure: very slim with long limbs and torso and chiseled arms. Rather than conventionally pretty, she was exotic and slightly otherworldly, with her square face, wide-set hazel eyes, and dark brown hair. She had enormous hands and feet (size 10A), but still seemed very feminine. She had not yet become the woman we remember today—she had frizzy hair—though she had already developed her distinctly girlish, breathless voice.

In the fall of 1947, Jackie enrolled at Vassar College—the

oldest of the Seven Sister schools. The student body at the time consisted largely of the daughters of privileged East Coast families. Jackie had scored in the ninetieth percentile on her college aptitude test and had been accepted at several colleges, but she chose Vassar for the simple reason that most of her friends were going there. Vassar's bucolic campus, situated on the outskirts of Poughkeepsie, New York, was just a two-hour drive from New York City, and Jackie's father was thrilled that she had chosen a college so close by. He looked forward to spending more time with her but also believed—mistakenly—that it signaled a subtle shift in her allegiance away from the Auchincloss family and back to him.

At Vassar, Jackie's two favorite courses were a history of religion and a lecture series on Shakespeare. A good student, she made the dean's list in both her freshman and sophomore years, and her friends described her as intellectually curious and very well read. But even at age eighteen, Jackie seemed enigmatic.

She was very shy and modest, rarely mentioning her debutante title or her high grades. Yet she had a presence that others couldn't help but notice, and a reticence that lent her a certain air of mystery. Friends say that Jackie was very private even in college. When her girlfriends got together for late-night chats, she revealed few details about herself, her family, or the men she was dating. She kept a picture of her father in her dormitory room and her girlfriends would often comment on his handsome, leading-man looks, but Jackie rarely volunteered any information about him. Although she loved his wild streak, perhaps as she matured, she became more aware of the price it exacted. To many of her classmates, Jackie seemed to float through Vassar while keeping everyone at arm's length. She was not involved in any extracurricular activities and often left campus on the weekends to visit one of the men's colleges or attend a debutante function. Her popularity had increased dramatically after she was named Debutante of the Year, and she was besieged with requests for dates. On weekends when she wasn't socializing, she visited her father in New York or went home to Merrywood.

Jackie's father was upset that his daughter was constantly going off to Harvard and Yale for romantic weekends, preferring that she be more involved in extracurricular activities. He was also deeply hurt that Jackie didn't spend more time with him. He complained to friends and relatives that his daughter only visited when she needed money, and on several occasions he threatened to withhold her allowance if she didn't visit more often.

Once, after a weekend away at Yale, Jackie didn't make it back in time for her curfew at Vassar. She received an angry letter from her father, warning her to protect her reputation. Obviously worried about his daughter's judgment, in subsequent letters he impressed on her how important it was to play hard to get with men. He even used his own experience as an example, saying that he would always lose interest in a woman who responded too quickly to his advances.

According to her college friends, Jackie's father didn't have much to worry about. They remember Jackie as being very selective about her dates and not very serious about any of her boyfriends. Chris O'Donnell, one of her suitors at the time, told David Heymann that "Jackie was never sexually adventuresome. The minute you'd turn into her driveway after a date, she'd tell the taxidriver to hold the meter. 'Hold your meter, driver.' You knew you weren't getting past the front door."

College friends also remember that Jackie had very little interest in politics, even in 1948—a particularly exciting election year. During the primaries, Progressive Henry Wallace and Dixiecrat Strom Thurmond both challenged fellow Democrat and incumbent Harry Truman. After a rough few months, Truman secured the nomination and then waged a neck-and-neck campaign against Republican candidate Thomas Dewey. Jackie's college classmates, like much of the country, were engrossed in the race—Truman edged out Dewey in the end—but Jackie showed no signs of interest.

In January 1948, Jackie's paternal grandfather died, and Jackie's father was dealt a crushing financial blow. He had been anticipating a substantial inheritance, but he was left nothing in the will. Jack's father felt that the money he had loaned his son, which was never repaid, exceeded his share of the estate. Jackie, along with the other Bouvier grandchildren, received $3,000 each in trust.

That summer, rather than vacationing in the Hamptons with her father as usual, Jackie went on a tour of Europe with three girlfriends, chaperoned by a teacher from Holton Arms. Over a period of seven weeks they visited England, France, Switzerland, and Italy.

By the end of her sophomore year, Jackie was disenchanted with Vassar and its all-female student body, and seriously contemplated dropping out to become a photographer's model. Although impractical, this was not some absurd teenage fantasy. Jackie had done occasional amateur modeling for charity fashion shows and had once received a token sum for appearing in *Life* magazine when they covered a Vassar charity show. But Jackie quickly dropped this plan after reading an advertisement for a "study abroad" program that offered students a chance to take their junior year in Paris.

Jackie left for France in the middle of August 1949. She spent her first weeks in a French immersion course at the

Elizabeth Curth, Margaret Snyder, Jackie, Mary Ann Freedman, and Hester Williams on the De Grasse, *sailing to France.*

University of Grenoble, then journeyed on to Paris to study at the Sorbonne. She wanted to avoid the sterile confines of Reid Hall, the dormitory where most of the American students resided, and chose instead to board with a French family who let rooms to students. Jackie's landlady, Countess Guyot de Renty, and her husband had fought in the French underground during World War II until they were captured, deported to Germany, and thrown into separate concentration camps. Her husband did not survive. After the war the countess and her two daughters returned to Paris.

Although later in life Jackie would be known for her expensive tastes, she loved her modest living quarters in Paris. The countess, her two daughters, her grandchild, two other American students, and Jackie all lived in a cramped apartment at 78 Avenue Mozart in the 12th arrondissement. There was no central heating. Seven people shared one bathroom, which had both an antique tub and a shower but rarely any hot water. In 1949, postwar food rationing was still in effect. To purchase milk and other scarce staples, Jackie, like native Parisians, had to present a ration card. It was indeed an enormous change from the world that Jackie had left behind, but Jackie adored living with the de Rentys, who provided the warm and loving atmosphere that had been missing in her youth.

Even when she was alone in France, Jackie did not entirely escape the influence of her parents. Her mother insisted on constant contact, and Jackie joked that when she didn't write every week, her mother "gets hysterical and thinks I'm dead or married to an Italian." While away, Jackie also had some reason to be anxious about her financial situation back home. In Paris, she received a letter from stepbrother Yusha Auchincloss, who revealed that the family was considering selling Merrywood because the estate had become too expensive to maintain. According to John Davis, during this year abroad Jackie decided to visit her father's former girlfriend in England to see the twins he had allegedly fathered. Afterward she wrote to her father that there was an incredible likeness between him and the children, and she was convinced that he was indeed the father. The twins both died in fluke accidents, but their existence haunted Jackie for years to come. (As the wife of a political candidate she feared this unseemly fact would be used against her by one of her husband's political opponents.)

Jackie was enchanted by Paris. She enjoyed her French literature and history courses at the Sorbonne, and liked visiting the Louvre and hanging out on the Left Bank at famous Hemingway haunts such as Café de Flore and Les Deux Magots. She dated several socially prominent American men who were spending time in Paris. One was future writer George Plimpton. He and Jackie remained good friends for the rest of her life. Another was John Phillips Marquand, Jr., whom everyone called Jack. Jackie fell in love with the witty, Harvard-educated Marquand, who at that time was following in his father's footsteps by writing a novel. Marquand's father, John Phillips Marquand, Sr. created the fictional detective Mr. Moto, and won the Pulitzer Prize for his novel *The Late George Aply*. It has been reported that Jackie surrendered her virginity to Marquand while they were in an elevator that stalled on the way up to his apartment, a claim that Marquand has denied.

"I loved it more than any year of my life," she told *Vogue* magazine in 1951. Her time in Paris also proved to be an enormous political asset. Her knowledge of French culture and command of the language would captivate Charles de Gaulle and the citizens of France during her legendary trip to Paris with John Kennedy in 1961. It was also in Paris that Jackie developed her sense of style. Ironically, her role model was Audrey Hepburn, whose role in the movie *Sabrina* was that of a poor American girl who reinvented herself in Paris and returned home a knockout.

After this heady year, Jackie found the thought of returning to Vassar and the little industrial town of Poughkeepsie abhorrent. Instead, she decided to complete her senior year at George Washington University in Washington, D.C. For Jackie, GW was just a place to finish up college and get a degree. When she graduated in 1951 with a degree in French literature, she didn't even bother to have her picture taken for the yearbook.

JACKIE'S *VOGUE* ESSAY

As a senior at George Washington University, Jackie entered *Vogue*'s annual Prix de Paris writing contest. She was asked to submit several essays on fashion-related topics as well as a biographical essay and an essay on famous people that she wished she had known. Jackie won, beating over twelve hundred other contestants.

From her personal profile:

"As to physical appearance, I am tall, 5′ 7″, with brown hair, a square face, and eyes so unfortunately far apart that it takes three weeks to have a pair of glasses made with a bridge wide enough to fit over my nose. I do not have a sensational figure but can look slim if I pick the right clothes. I flatter myself on being able at times to walk out of the house looking like the poor man's Paris copy, but often my mother will run up to inform me that my left stocking seam is crooked or the right-hand topcoat button is about to fall off. This, I realize, is the Unforgivable Sin."

From an essay wherein she devised a beauty regimen for a college girl:

"You can never slip into too dismal an abyss of untidiness if once every seven days you will pull yourself up short and cope with ragged ends. . . . If you will allot two hours as sacrosanct as any of your classes, you can avoid smudged nails daubed on the New York Central from a bottle of polish that has spilled in your pocketbook, strange unwanted waves in your hair because you have washed it at midnight and gone to bed too tired to wait for it to dry, stubbly legs with razor cuts, and a legion of other horrors. . . ."

From "People I wish I had known":

"I would say that the three men I should most like to have known were Charles Baudelaire, Oscar Wilde, and Serge Diaghileff. . . .

"Baudelaire and Wilde were both rich men's sons who lived like dandies, ran through what they had, and died in extreme poverty. Both were poets and idealists who could paint sinfulness with honesty and still believed in something higher. . . . Serge Diaghileff dealt not with an interaction of the senses but with the interaction of the arts, an interaction of the cultures of East and West. Though not an artist himself, he possessed what is rarer than artistic genius in any one field, the sensitivity to take the best of each man and incorporate it into the masterpiece all the more precious because it lives only in the minds of those who have seen it and disintegrates as soon as he is gone. . . ."

Her year at George Washington would have been altogether uneventful except for one thing: winning the *Vogue* Prix de Paris, a writing contest for college seniors sponsored by the magazine. All applicants had to submit a personal profile, several essays on fashion-related topics, and an essay titled "People I Wish I Had Known." First prize was a one-year position with *Vogue* as a junior editor—six months in the magazine's New York offices and six months in its Paris bureau. Jackie was determined to win and spent all of her free time working on her submission, which beat out twelve hundred others. Cleverly composed and stylishly written, her essays are still to this day perhaps the best evidence of her intellectual ability.

Jackie entered the *Vogue* contest at her mother's suggestion, but when she won, her mother begged her to turn down the prize. Janet felt her daughter had spent too much time in Europe and was afraid that if she were to go back she might never come home. More worrying to Janet perhaps was the fact that Jackie might marry Marquand. According to Klein, she knew Jackie was in love with him, but she didn't believe a writer would ever make enough money to support her daughter. As a consolation prize, Hugh and Janet Auchincloss promised to send Jackie and Lee to Europe—but just for one summer, and only if she turned down the *Vogue* offer.

But Jackie decided to defy her mother. Ignoring her mother's pleas, she went to New York to begin her internship. She only lasted a week—for reasons that today sound odd: Her mother convinced her that *Vogue* was not the place to meet eligible young men. "Mark my words," Janet Auchincloss warned, "you're making the biggest mistake of your life. You're going to be twenty-two years old in July, and you're not engaged yet."

Jackie formally declined the *Vogue* prize but was left with a dilemma: What was she going to do with her life? Before she won the *Vogue* contest, she had been offered an entry-level job at the CIA, but that didn't interest her. Her father suggested that she work for him part-time in his brokerage firm, where she would meet many young men with prospects. Her mother, however, wanted her to come home so she could watch over her daughter and ensure that she meet the right kind of man.

She was finally convinced to come home from New York when Hugh Auchincloss promised that when she returned from her trip with Lee, he would help her find a job as a journalist in Washington. Jackie declined the prize, then went to Europe with Lee. It was Lee's first trip, and Jackie acted as her tour guide and chaperone. They sailed on the *Queen Elizabeth* to England, and in France they hung around with the friends Jackie had made while at the Sorbonne. Jackie became very interested in art and, in Venice, took sketching lessons from an Italian artist. The sisters stayed briefly at I Tatti, the estate of art critic and collector Bernard Berenson, just outside Florence. Berenson gave Jackie some advice, not about painting but about the art of finding a husband: "Marry someone who will constantly stimulate you—and you him."

"Are you still hiring little girls?"

Hugh Auchincloss kept his end of the bargain. When Jackie returned from Europe, he asked his close friend Arthur Krock, then a Washington correspondent for the *New York*

INQUIRING CAMERA GIRL

JACKIE BEHIND THE CAMERA.

In the early 1950s, Jackie Bouvier worked in Washington, D.C., earning $42.40 a week as the "inquiring photographer" for the *Washington Times-Herald*. Her job was to roam the city, stopping people at random on the street, interviewing them briefly, and then taking their pictures.

Not all her interview subjects were unknown. Jackie would also track down the capital's famous residents and ask them offbeat questions. Once she went to Duke Zeibert's, one of the city's best-known restaurants, and asked the chef, Jou Kerriou, what he

would serve a man for his last meal. "A vodka martini, turtle soup, Châteaubriand, and a Grand Marnier soufflé with Napoleon brandy," Kerriou replied. In one of her columns she asked her subjects to reveal their "secret ambition." Newspaper columnist Arthur Krock's answer revealed his obsession with journalism. "Just once before I die," Krock told Jackie, "I'd like to turn out an article in which every sentence would be clear, well-balanced, and concise." In 1952, the year Richard Nixon was first elected vice president, she went to Nixon's residence and interviewed then six-year-old Tricia about her father. "He's always away," said the little girl. "If he's famous, why can't he stay home? . . . All my class was voting for Eisenhower but I told them I was just going to vote for Daddy."

Some of her questions had a literary bent and seemed designed to provoke. "Noël Coward said that women should be struck regularly like gongs." She would then ask, Do you agree? Citing Chaucer, who said that what women most desire is power over men, she inquired, What do you think women most desire? Do you consider yourself normal? Do you think your life story would make a good movie? Would you like to crash high society?

For one of her columns about political life in Washington, she interviewed Vice President Nixon and Senator John F. Kennedy. After becoming involved with Kennedy, her questions began to reveal a preoccupation with marriage: Do you think men are just as anxious to get married as women? Do you think a wife should let her husband think he's smarter than she is? What advice would you give girls to find a husband before leap year is over? Are wives a necessity or a luxury?

As Jackie biographer David Heymann points out, questions having to do with being president or First Lady, dating Marilyn Monroe,

and fashion in the White House now seem prescient. "Her questions, looked at retrospectively," says Jackie author Wayne Koestenbaum, "seem part of a premeditated scheme, as if Jackie, holding her Graflex camera and asking innocuous questions, were planting clues about her personality."

Jackie's questions might have been interesting, but her work received mixed reviews from her colleagues. Some of her fellow journalists said she was a hard worker and that she improved the column. But others claimed she was inexperienced and unable to come up with any of her own ideas. They felt she only kept the job because of her connections. "Her looks were her main contribution to the newsroom," said one reporter. Jackie's ethical standards were questionable, as her half sister, Nina Auchincloss, inadvertently revealed years later. She claimed that Jackie would ask friends and family members to dress up in disguises and be interviewed as stand-ins when things were going slowly on the street.

In an article in the *Washingtonian* magazine, editor Frank Waldrop summed up Jackie's ability and performance. "She worked hard at the paper, never whined or ratted," he said. "She was ambitious. She was neat and nice and businesslike. She's a good example of a youngster who takes advantage of her opportunities."

Times, if he could help Jackie find an entry-level position at a paper. Krock called his friend Frank Waldrop, editor-in-chief and part owner of the now defunct *Washington Times-Herald*. "Are you still hiring little girls?" Krock asked. "I have a wonder for you. She's round-eyed, clever, and wants to go into journalism." He managed to work into the conversation that the "little girl" in question was the stepdaughter of the well-known Hugh Auchincloss. Waldrop agreed to meet her.

During their interview, Waldrop asked Jackie if she was really interested in a career in journalism or just passing time until she got married. Jackie assured him of her long-term commitment to the profession and clinched the deal. She started as a gofer, but after a few weeks Waldrop sent her to see Sid Epstein, the city editor who was looking for a new inquiring photographer. The job consisted of going out into the streets, buttonholing passersby, and printing their pictures. Epstein was initially reluctant, saying that he wanted an experienced reporter.

To change Epstein's mind, Jackie protested that she had some photography experience and knew how to work a Leica. Epstein mockingly explained that at the *Times-Herald* they used a Speed Graphic, a more unwieldy and complicated camera than a Leica. But he said that if she could learn to use it by the next day she could have the job. A photographer was then assigned to explain the basics of operating a Speed Graphic. It was clear to everyone in the newsroom that Jackie was very amateurish, to say the least. To show her how far she should stand from her subjects, a six-foot-tall reporter had to lie down on the floor of the newsroom. But Epstein was impressed with Jackie's drive and gave her the job. Her starting salary was $42.50 a week.

Perhaps frightened by her mother's warning that if she

didn't marry soon she would become an old maid, when Jackie returned from Europe she began dating several different men—and uncharacteristically—got very serious with one of them. A few days after she started her new job at the *Times-Herald*, she formally announced her engagement. Her fiancé's name was John. John G. W. Husted, Jr.

1953

CHAPTER THREE

MARRIAGE

John G. W. Husted, Jr., was a tall, handsome Waspy Yale graduate with a job at Dominick and Dominick, a top investment bank in New York. As soon as he met Jackie he was smitten. Within weeks, Husted proposed over the telephone, telling her to meet him at the fashionable Polo Bar at the Westbury Hotel at noon on Saturday if she was willing to marry him.

While very fond of Husted, Jackie exhibited from the start a certain ambivalence about a long-term relationship with him. At the appointed hour, Jackie didn't arrive, but Husted decided to give her a little leeway, as there was a terrible snowstorm in New York that day. He waited for three hours. Just as he was about to leave, Jackie waltzed in as if she was right on time. She accepted Husted's proposal, and he presented her with a diamond and sapphire ring that had belonged to his mother. The engagement was announced in the *New York Times* on January 21, 1952. The couple was to be married in June of that year.

One cause of Jackie's hesitancy might have been her mother's disapproval. Janet didn't think Husted was wealthy enough to be a suitable husband for her daughter. Although Husted made a decent salary—about $17,000 a year—and came from a family of respectably well-off bankers, Janet thought her attractive, well-educated daughter could do better, and Jackie seemed to be of the same opinion. Though she had always joked that her only requirements for a boyfriend were that he "weigh more and have bigger feet than I do," when faced with the prospect of marrying Husted, her standards suddenly rose. Money remained a crucial issue, but she had other concerns, too. Jackie was enamored of charismatic, dangerous men— men like her father, Black Jack—and Husted was dependable, quiet, unassuming, maybe even a bit bland; according to friends, there was little chemistry between the two. A guest who attended an engagement party the Auchinclosses threw early in the year for the young couple reported that "they hardly spoke to each other, and when they did, Jackie would merely nod her head and smile."

She was also caught up in her new journalism job, was enjoying meeting new people, and soon grew tired of commuting between Washington and New York on the weekends so that she and her fiancé could spend time together.

Louis Auchincloss, writer and relative, who was introduced to Jackie's fiancé at a family gathering one evening, told Ed Klein that he knew the match wouldn't last. "What no one seemed to have known about Jackie at that time," said Auchincloss, "was that she wasn't this soft little girlish person. She was very tough. Very tough. The major motivation in her life was money. She loved money. And I had the curious conviction that this whole evening wasn't real, that her whole destiny would be different. A very different destiny."

His instincts were correct. As the months went by, Jackie opted to spend more and more of her weekends in Washington. She threw lavish parties at Merrywood, inviting many of the influential political, business, and journalistic figures she met through work. She even began casually dating other men, spending lots of time with Godfrey McHugh, an Air Force officer ten years her senior, as well as William Walton, a *Time* correspondent.

Then John Kennedy appeared on the scene, or in point of fact reappeared. The two were not complete strangers. In May 1951 Martha Bartlett, the wife of Jackie's close friend and journalist Charles Bartlett, had been annoyed that her husband was spending so much time with Jackie. Desperately wanting to introduce Jackie to an eligible man, she threw a dinner party at her Georgetown home with the intention of setting Jackie up with John Kennedy.

Twelve years older than Jackie, Jack Kennedy was a member of Congress from the 11th Congressional District of Massachussetts while she was still finishing up at GW. Despite the age difference, however, the two seemed to hit it off. Jackie was impressed with the charming, self-confident politician, and Jack, who generally dated somewhat "faster" women, seemed quite taken with her beauty and intelligence. He was interested enough to call the Bartletts the following day to inquire about her, but he never followed up. Within the next year, Jackie was engaged to Husted. When the Bartletts became aware that she wasn't entirely devoted to her new fiancé, they encouraged her to invite Jack Kennedy to escort her to another of their dinner parties. At the time, Kennedy was waging a senatorial campaign in Massachussetts against Republican incumbent Henry Cabot Lodge. Once again he and Jackie took to each other, and this time Jack made sure to follow up. After their first date at the Shoreham Hotel's Blue Room, where they danced while their "chaperon"—Kennedy political aide Dave Powers—kept watch, the two began seeing each other sporadically.

Jackie was entirely captivated with the rakish, extroverted playboy. Husted had come from a family that traveled in the same circles as the Auchinclosses, but that didn't guarantee financial security. Even though the Kennedys weren't from the same social stratum, they had money: Jack had a $10 million trust fund, and the family's fortune was estimated by *Forbes* at $400 million. John Kennedy also had the potential to build further on his already successful political career. In 1952, less than a year after he and Jackie began seeing each other, he was elected senator from Massachusetts. Jackie may not have been particularly interested in politics, but Jack's power and prospects impressed her.

Husted, meanwhile, was not unaware that Jackie's feelings for him were changing. He told biographer David Heymann that immediately following their engagement, Jackie's letters to him were extremely passionate, but as time went on, they became markedly less so. Eventually Husted received a guilty-sounding note from Jackie: "Don't listen to any of the drivel you hear about me and Jack Kennedy." Shortly thereafter he received another letter in which Jackie claimed that her mother was concerned they were rushing into marriage and suggested they reschedule the wedding.

In April 1952 Jackie finally mustered the courage to end her halfhearted relationship with Husted. She broke the news during one of his weekend visits to Merrywood. "You're one of the nicest kindest people in the world," Jackie told him. "But I may not be the most appropriate person for you. I'm thinking of your future happiness, John, not mine." On Sunday before

Husted boarded the plane to return to New York, Jackie removed her engagement ring and put it in his jacket pocket. No words were spoken. Husted wrote to Jackie hoping to convince her that she was making a terrible mistake. She wrote back that her decision was final.

Now that Jackie was truly eligible and Jack had won his Senate campaign, they began to date more seriously, frequently attending dinner parties at the homes of close friends, such as Senator and Mrs. Albert Gore, where they played board games, bridge, and charades. They also spent lots of time with Bobby Kennedy and his wife, Ethel, at their home in Georgetown. Sexually, Jackie was more adventurous with Jack than she had been with Husted. Once, a state trooper interrupted the couple while they were necking in Jack's convertible on a secluded road outside of Washington. Unaware that the male culprit was a senator, the trooper shone his flashlight at the car; Jack was half naked and had removed Jackie's brassiere. Once the trooper recognized Senator Kennedy, he apologized and backed off.

As a celebrity member of Congress, Jack was unquestionably a bigger "catch" than Husted, but he also had bigger drawbacks. A notorious womanizer, he was also vain and immature. Jackie told her cousin John Davis that Jack "goes to a hairdresser almost every day to have his hair done so that it'll always look bushy and fluffy," and that if "we go out to a party or reception or something where nobody recognizes him, or no photographer takes his picture, he sulks afterward for hours."

He had other shortcomings, too. A slipped disc in his back caused constant, severe pain, and he also had a potentially fatal disease, Addison's disease, a dysfunction of the adrenal glands that eventually destroys the immune system. Perhaps because he was plagued by pain, he had a volatile temper—which was often unleashed on Jackie. Although not punctual himself, he berated Jackie if she ever kept him waiting. He was not particularly warm, nor was he a thoughtful suitor, never sending Jackie gifts and rarely complimenting her.

Jackie was rather cold and detached herself. She confided to John Davis that she and Jack had similar dispositions: Both were like "icebergs," with large parts of their personalities "submerged." She decided that Jack was worth the heartbreak she might endure and made up her mind to pursue him with a vengeance. Her interest in a newspaper career, once so strong, began to wane. Now she concentrated on convincing Jack that she would be a suitable wife. She edited reports and ran errands, helped him shop for clothes, accompanied him to political dinners, and regularly brought warm lunches to his office. She pretended that they liked the same activities, even feigning interest in the lowbrow adventure films and Westerns Jack dragged her to see. "What I want more than anything else in the world is to marry Jack Kennedy," she confided to a friend.

On July 4, 1952, Jack finally took his new girlfriend to Hyannis Port on Cape Cod to meet his family. Jackie realized how influential they would be in his decision to marry, and knew that this was a test of sorts—and one that would not be easy to pass. The Kennedys were completely unlike her own family: Tightly knit, loud, overbearing, and fiercely competitive, they were always involved in some athletic activity—tennis or touch football—or engrossed in heated political discussions. Jackie was initially intoxicated by their energy and vitality. "How can I explain these people? They were like carbonated water, and other families might be flat," she later told a reporter.

Jackie, with Jack and his sister-in-law Ethel, in Georgetown.

But however much she admired their high spirits, she clearly did not fit in. Jackie was poised and polished, the Kennedys rough and uncouth. Jack's sisters Eunice, Jean, and Pat, together with Bobby's wife, Ethel, relentlessly teased their brother's girlfriend and made fun of her affected high-society manner. When Jackie announced that her name was pronounced "Jac-lean," Eunice whispered cattily to her sisters,

"Rhymes with queen." They called her "The Deb," mimicked her childlike breathless way of speaking, and tormented her for refusing to eat the peanut butter and jelly sandwiches they had made for one of their sailing excursions, packing pâté, quiche, and a bottle of white wine instead.

Although an experienced equestrienne, Jackie had very little knowledge of or interest in the contact sports that were an everyday occurrence at Hyannis Port. Jack's sisters chided her for not knowing which way to run in a football game. In response, she dubbed them the "rah-rah" girls, complaining to her own sister, Lee, that they were so undignified that "they would fall over each other like a pack of gorillas." After twisting her ankle in a touch football game, Jackie told Lee, "They'll kill me before I ever get to marry him. I swear they will." She tried to put an end to the hectic activity she was forced to participate in. "It's enough for me to enjoy a sport without having to win, place, or show," she told Jack.

Rose Kennedy also came to think of Jackie as pretentious and ridiculed her habit of turning on the faucet in the bathroom so nobody would hear her using the toilet and was irritated when she slept in. But Jackie did, however, have a staunch protector in the family patriarch, Joe Kennedy. She knew that if Joe wanted his son to marry her, a proposal would be imminent, and shrewdly cultivated that relationship, chatting and joking with Jack's father constantly. Although the Kennedys were extremely wealthy, Jackie knew that they suffered from a social inferiority complex. Joe had never been fully able to penetrate the snobbish crowd of Boston Brahmins who surrounded him, and was determined that his children would marry people of higher social standing. Jackie played on his insecurity, constantly making references to her "elite" French Catholic ancestry (which was, in fact, not terribly aristocratic). And although in reality Jackie had very little money, she acted as though she had limitless resources.

It's somewhat unclear whether Joe Kennedy knew she was embellishing her pedigree, but it probably wouldn't have mattered to the man who often said, "It's not what you are that counts. It's what people think you are." Jackie definitely seemed to have the right qualifications to marry Jack. "A politician has to have a wife, and a Catholic politician has to have a Catholic wife," Joe Kennedy told a friend of Jack's. "She should have class. Jackie has more class than any girl we've ever seen around here."

Jackie took Jack to New York to meet her own father. The meeting went well. According to Jackie, the two men in her life "talked about sports, politics, and women—what all red-blooded men like to talk about." They also commiserated over the back pain that plagued them both.

Like a textbook fifties flirt, Jackie tried her best to "manage" her man. She played hard to get, feigning indifference when he took out other women and making sure that he knew she, too, was dating. But Jackie began to wonder how much more time she should put into this cat-and-mouse game when her younger sister, Lee, beat her to the altar and married Michael Canfield, the adopted son of Harper & Brothers publisher Cass Canfield. At their wedding on April 18, 1953, Lee tossed her bouquet directly to Jackie. Jack must have realized that his girlfriend's patience was wearing thin; the following month, he proposed.

The formal announcement of their engagement was delayed because the *Saturday Evening Post* had written an article about Jack titled "The Senate's Gay Young Bachelor," and Jack wanted to remain a bachelor at least until the piece hit the newsstands. In the meantime, his secret fiancée planned a

THE KENNEDY FAMILY

By the 1960s, the Kennedys had become American royalty, but their roots were hardly noble. Jack Kennedy's great-grandfather had fled the Irish potato famine. Within a generation, the family was involved in politics. His grandfather was Boston ward heeler P. J. Kennedy, who was well enough off to vacation in Florida and send his son Joe to Harvard, the bastion of establishment education. Just a few years out of college, Joe became a bank presi-dent and began building his for-tune. He invested heavily, and suc-cessfully, in Hollywood, and during the Prohibition era, made millions running illegal bootlegging busi-nesses. Despite the ties to the Mob that he developed as a bootlegger and Hollywood financier, and his isolationist views, Joe Kennedy was named head of the Securities and Exchange Commission by President Franklin D. Roosevelt as well as U.S. Ambassador to the Court of St. James.

Joe married up when he took the hand of Rose Fitzgerald, the eldest daughter of Boston mayor John Francis Fitzgerald. Rose bore Joe nine children—Joseph, Jr., John,

Rosemary, Kathleen, Eunice, Patricia, Robert, Jean Ann, and Edward. There were so many children that Rose had to keep three-by-five-inch card files on each of them to remember their medications, clothes, and other vital statistics. Rose was a strict disciplinarian who, together with her husband, fostered a highly competitive environment in the home. All the children were required to take swimming, tennis, sailing, and golf lessons and then to compete among themselves. Winning was everything. She reserved her soft side for just one of her children, Rosemary, who had been born retarded and, in later life, was given a needless prefrontal lobotomy on her father's orders and placed in a sanitarium, while he pretended to the world that she had become a nun.

Joe was a controlling father who always felt slighted by the Protestant establishment. His greatest desire was to ensure that his children conquered a world that had never quite accepted him. He was also an incorrigible womanizer. He would shamelessly make passes at his daughters' schoolmates and his sons' girlfriends, and would thoughtlessly bring his mistresses along on family outings. He would brag about his affairs, often within earshot of long-suffering Rose, who once actually left him, only to return. Joe's most famous dalliance was with the actress Gloria Swanson. Joe encouraged his own sons to emulate his behavior with women. He would leave pornographic magazines on their beds and would disparage women as little more than sex objects in front of them.

Few would have chosen Jack as the future president in the family, including his father. He was an immensely sickly child—coming down with scarlet fever, whooping cough, measles, chicken pox, German measles, tonsillitis, bronchitis, ear infections, and anemia. His constant illness left him with hours of time alone, which he spent reading. Nor was Jack particularly handsome as a boy. Skinny and drawn from sickness, he had angular features that earned him the nickname "Rat Face" at school.

Joe, Jr., not Jack, was the model child—funny, charismatic, strong, and handsome. His father consciously groomed him for a future in politics. During World War II, Jack skippered PT-109. Jack's heroic feats made headlines everywhere. Out of envy, Joe volunteered for a dangerous bombing mission against a German submarine base. He never came back. Years later, Jack's favorite sister, Kathleen, died in a plane crash with her fiancé. Buffeted by tragedy, Joe, Sr. turned to Jack as the son who would have to fulfill his father's grand ambitions.

vacation with her friend Aileen Bowdoin, who had snagged invitations to the coronation of Elizabeth II in England. When the *Times-Herald* learned that Jackie had gotten access to this event, they asked her to cover it for the paper. She wrote celebrity stories about the parties she attended there and did one article on the commoners' view of the coronation. Knowing that Jackie was a competent artist, the paper also asked her to submit some sketches of the coronation and published them on the front page of the paper.

It was her final moment in the journalistic spotlight, and she got Jack's attention. He sent a telegram that read, "ARTI-CLES EXCELLENT, BUT YOU ARE MISSED"—a rare romantic gesture. While abroad, however, Jackie began to have some doubts. She had spent so much time focusing on how to get him to propose that she hadn't actually thought much beyond the betrothal. She stayed on in Europe, spending an extra two weeks in Paris trying to sort out her feelings. She was aware of Jack's philandering. "How can you live with a husband who is bound to be unfaithful but whom one loves?" she asked a friend. Becoming part of the Kennedy family and the incredible demands they would put on her also made her pause. In the end, her doubts subsided and she decided to accept Jack's proposal.

❦ ❦ ❦

". . .this relationship will take a lot of working out."

On her flight back home, Jackie sat near actress Zsa Zsa Gabor. Zsa Zsa later remembered, "Twenty-four hours on the plane she kept asking me—it was no joke—'What do you do for your skin?'" Jackie was not aware that the actress had previously had an affair with Jack Kennedy, who was waiting for Jackie at the airport. When Jack saw Zsa Zsa he ran up to her and the two embraced. Moments later, Jackie came upon them. Jack introduced Jackie to Zsa Zsa. "Miss Bouvier and I spent hours on the plane," Zsa Zsa explained. "She's a lovely girl. Don't dare corrupt her, Jack." Jackie replied, "But he already has."

The engagement was formally announced on June 24, 1953, and it made headlines across the country. "Hopeful debutantes from Washington to Boston, from Palm Beach to Hollywood, can begin unpacking their hope chests" reported the *New York Daily News*. Jack gave his fiancée a twinned, square-cut, emerald and diamond engagement ring from Van Cleef and Arpels. But he was not the one who went to the Fifth Avenue store to select the ring—it was his father, Joe.

The burdensome responsibilities of marrying a politician made themselves immediately apparent. A week after they were engaged, Jackie returned to Hyannis Port for a leisurely vacation, having quit her job at the *Times-Herald*. When she arrived she was surprised to see *Life* magazine photographer Hy Peskin at the compound, waiting to take her picture. Without Jackie's consent, Jack had agreed that he and his future bride would cooperate for a July 20, 1953, *Life* spread on their engagement titled "SENATOR KENNEDY GOES A-COURTIN'." When Jackie expressed her concern, his family told her that she would have to do it for the good of Jack's career.

The onslaught of press had begun. Reporters constantly asked her about her relationship with Jack. Once when she was asked by a reporter whether they shared anything in common, she replied that they had "too much" in common. "Since Jack is such a violently independent person, and I, too, am so independent, this relationship will take a lot of working out," she said.

But her own "violent independence" would be curbed by political considerations. Both Jackie and her mother wanted a small, exclusive wedding with no reporters, but the Kennedys insisted on a big affair with lots of press coverage. Usually formidable, Janet Auchincloss was no match for the tough-as-nails Joe Kennedy. A big wedding was scheduled for September 12, 1953.

Janet Auchincloss was not impressed by Joe Kennedy. She thought him rude and vulgar and told friends that Jackie was marrying beneath her. She was also alarmed when in August, only weeks before the wedding, her daughter's fiancé decided to go for what he called a last fling on a Mediterranean cruise with a college roommate. She warned Jackie that it wasn't the act of a man in love. Jackie, though concerned about the trip herself, rationalized that it might be a good way for him to get womanizing out of his system before their marriage.

The wedding took place at St. Mary's in Newport on September 12, 1953, before more than 750 guests. The weather was perfect. Richard Cardinal Cushing peformed the ceremony, while 3,000 onlookers jostled outside the church for a better view. Bobby was best man, and Lee was matron of honor. Jack's face was scratched in a last-minute game of touch football before the ceremony, but apparently it wasn't noticeable. At one point, Jack joked that he was marrying Jackie just to get rid of a member of the press.

The reception was held afterward, at Hammersmith Farm. Tents were set up on the lawn, and the 1,300 guests danced to the Meyer Davis band, the same band that had played at Black Jack and Janet's wedding. Jack and Jackie chose "I Married an

THE WEDDING

THE WEDDING AT ST. MARY'S IN NEWPORT, R.I.

Newport had filed in on the bride's side, and the Kennedys were on the groom's side," recalled Newport resident and guest Marion "Oatsie" Leiter to Ed Klein. "Newport was dressed only a little better than if they'd been to the beach for lunch— neat linen dresses. The Kennedys were dressed to the nines, like chic new money." As for the bride, Jackie wore an ivory-colored gown that was made from fifty yards of taffeta, her grandmother's rose point lace veil, and a blue garter for good luck. She carried a bouquet of pink and white spray orchids, stephanotis, and miniature gardenias. Jackie had wanted to wear something that was simple and elegant, but her husband encouraged her to opt for an old-fashioned frilly wedding gown, which one critic derided as "an atrocious mass of tissue silk taffeta" and which Jackie herself felt was not flattering.

The dress had been designed by Anne Lowe, an African American who had a reputation for making expensive-looking dresses for upper-class women at reasonable prices. A few days before the wedding, there was a flood at Anne's workshop in New York City, and the wedding dress, as well as several bridesmaids' dresses, were completely ruined. Lowe had to work through the night to redo the lost dresses. Frightened to tell Janet Auchincloss about the accident, she took a $2,200 loss on her work.

Angel" for their first dance. During the party Jackie cheerfully tossed her bouquet of flowers, making sure it was caught by her close friend Nancy Tuckerman. To the public, the wedding seemed like a fairy tale come true. The following morning the *New York Times* wrote that it "far surpassed the Astor-French wedding of 1943." But in reality, the event was distinctly less than perfect.

Jackie's father had been determined to be in top form for his favorite daughter's wedding. He tanned himself and exercised all through the summer, meticulously choosing his wardrobe for the special occasion, when hundreds of people would be watching him give his daughter away. But he was very anxious about the event as well, and when Janet did not invite him to attend the prewedding ceremonies, he retreated to his hotel room and began drinking. By the time his brothers-in-law went to retrieve him, he was dead drunk. Furious, Janet forbade her ex-husband to attend the event, declaring that she would not allow him to ruin Jackie's wedding. Hugh Auchincloss stepped in for Black Jack and walked Jackie down the aisle. Reporters were told that Jackie's biological father was ill.

One theory suggests that Janet, who despised Black Jack, intentionally tried to keep her husband from attending the wedding by allegedly sending Lee's ex-husband, Michael Canfield, to his hotel to get him plastered. "I'll never know the true story," says Jamie Auchincloss. "[Black Jack] was capable of getting drunk himself because he'd done it many, many times in the past. And the particular stress that his daughter's wedding in Auchincloss-land was going to cause would exacerbate it."

Jackie was tremendously disappointed that her father was not able to give her away, but hardly anyone was aware of her feelings. "Aside from the usual confusion and excitement," said one of the bridesmaids, "you would never have guessed that anything was wrong." Although perfectly composed throughout the wedding, when she went into her bedroom to change for her honeymoon journey, she burst into tears.

Not long after, she emerged from her room cool and composed as ever in a chic gray Chanel suit, thanked Hugh Auchincloss for filling in for her father, and climbed into a limousine. The crowd threw handfuls of confetti as the newly married couple drove off, beaming and waving, looking every inch the golden couple that Jackie—and so many others—wanted to believe they were.

Georgetown, 1957

CHAPTER FOUR

SENATOR'S WIFE

The newlyweds spent two nights at the Waldorf-Astoria in New York and then flew to Acapulco for a two-week honeymoon, where they took a pink villa that Jackie had longed to stay at ever since she'd first seen it on a trip to Acapulco with her mother and stepfather. Joe Kennedy knew the owner and had made all the arrangements.

When Jackie arrived in Acapulco, the first thing she did was write to her father to console him, saying that she forgave him for the incident at her wedding. She said she fully understood how difficult the situation had been for him and that even though he hadn't physically accompanied her down the aisle, he'd been with her in her thoughts.

After the wedding ceremony, Jackie joked that Jack probably already missed being a bachelor. She wasn't far off. At parties in Acapulco, he surrounded himself with beautiful young women while his bride watched from the sidelines, hurt and humiliated.

Jack and Jackie sailing off the coast of Cape Cod.

The first year of marriage was difficult. Instead of finding their own home, Jack and Jackie lived with his parents in Hyannis Port for the first few months of their marriage, while Jack commuted to Washington during the week. Jackie disliked the arrangement and encouraged her husband to find a Washington home as soon as possible. In November 1953 they finally rented a town house in Georgetown, at 3321 Dent Place.

But having their own house only partially alleviated some of Jackie's growing unhappiness. She found it difficult to adjust to her new role as a political wife, not least because she was a good deal younger than most of the other senators' spouses. Having given up any ambition to have a career of her own, there was not much else for her to do now besides trying to show Jack that she could manage a household and be a help to his career. She took cooking lessons and spent time decorating the house. The woman who just years before had claimed her ambition in life was not to be a housewife now appeared to have had a dramatic change of heart. "I'm an old-fashioned wife," she gushed to a reporter. "Housekeeping is a joy to me. When it all runs smoothly, when the food is good and the flowers look fresh, I have much satisfaction." She tried to do what she thought was expected of her and what she thought would make Jack proud: joining the Senate Red Cross committee, watching her husband's speeches on the Senate floor, attending political luncheons and Capitol Hill cocktail parties. She also joined a bridge club, took golf lessons, and even enrolled in some classes in American politics so she could be more knowledgeable about Jack's work.

Domestic life was, for Jackie, a solitary affair. Jack was rarely home, and when he was, the house was filled with his political cronies. He traveled constantly, giving speeches and attending late-night meetings. Jackie attempted to get closer to her husband by trying to involve herself in his work, thinking of ways to improve his public speaking skills and even packing his suitcases. But she still felt that she was on the periphery of Jack's real life, and she became depressed. Undoubtedly, the fear that some of these late-night meetings and out-of-town trips might not have been as business-oriented as Jack claimed added to her unhappiness. She began to chain-smoke and bite her fingernails. According to a friend, "After the first year they were together, Jackie was wandering around looking like a survivor of an airplane crash."

Increasingly, the two were learning to reinvent their lives for public consumption. Once, Jackie told a friend that her husband's most distinctive characteristic was his "curious inquiring mind that is always at work." She added, "If I were to draw him, I would draw this tiny body and an enormous head." This was a flattering way of articulating the sense of estrangement and inequality that was actually a source of pain to Jackie. It is also a highly ironic portrait of a man better known for his insatiable sexual appetite than for his thirst for knowledge. Perhaps Jackie herself was well aware of the irony. For his part, Jack once said that he would draw himself as a straight horizontal line but would draw Jackie as a wavy line. These descriptions also seem out of line with the truth, given the single-minded dedication with which Jackie pursued some of her goals. But each seemed to exaggerate certain qualities in the other that blinded them to other personality traits.

In June the lease expired on their Georgetown home, and they resumed a transient life, staying either in hotels or with one set of their parents. Jack's chronic back problems added to their troubles in that first year. He wore a brace and in May had to begin using crutches just to get around. According to George Smathers, then senator from Florida and an old friend of Jack's from the House, "[Jack] was so sick that if they would ring the bell for a quorum call . . . I would literally almost carry him down to the underground train that led to the chambers. . . . He never said anything, but you could see the pain etched in his face."

By October 1954 the pain became so acute that Jack checked into New York's Hospital for Special Surgery to see if anything could be done to help him. Intense discomfort did not, apparently, interfere with his sex drive. According to Anderson, a life-size picture of Marilyn Monroe clad in dark blue shorts and a white tennis shirt hung in his hospital room, upside down so that her legs were spread apart in the air. Since only family members were allowed to visit Jack in the hospital, the beautiful women who paraded in and out to see him all claimed to be his sisters.

The doctors' diagnosis was not promising. The only procedure that might alleviate his pain was an operation in which they would remove a metal disc that had been inserted in a previous operation and perform a double fusion of the spine. Jack's own doctors at the Lahey Clinic in Boston strongly advised him against it. It was a risky procedure for any patient, but for Jack, who had Addison's disease, it could be fatal. If he contracted an infection it was likely he would die.

Jackie was scared by the choice, but felt it should be Jack's. Joe, who feared he might lose yet another son, tried to persuade Jack not to go through with the operation. He told his son he could still have a fulfilling life and a successful political career even if confined to a wheelchair, pointing to FDR as an example. But Jack was adamant, saying once that he'd prefer dying to a life with crutches. The operation was performed on October 21, 1954, and as the doctors in Boston had feared, there were complications. Jack developed an infection and was in critical condition after the operation, falling into a coma from which it seemed unlikely he would ever recover. A priest administered his last rites.

Jackie, only twenty-five years old at the time, appeared to be on the verge of losing her husband. But rather than crumbling upon hearing the news, she seemed to snap out of her depression, and exhibited surprising strength and courage. She held her husband's hand and read poetry to him while he lay motionless. Jack's mother and sisters were finally impressed by Jackie. Under these tragic circumstances, she finally had what she long craved: undivided time with her husband, and the respect of his family.

Miraculously, Jack came out of the coma, but his condition remained life-threatening. Jackie was constantly by his side, attempting to nurse him back to health. She spoon-fed him, helped him wash and change into his bathrobe, kept him informed of all the Washingon gossip he felt he was missing, and sneaked candy into his room to satisfy his sweet tooth. One evening, she even smuggled in the actress Grace Kelly, disguised in a nurse's uniform. Jackie also wrote thank you notes to political colleagues who expressed concern about Jack's condition, including one remarkable letter to Richard Nixon, who was then vice president and who would soon run against Kennedy for the presidency. "I don't think there is anyone in the world [Jack] thinks more highly of than he does you," Jackie wrote.

After two months, Jack was still in great pain. They moved him to the Kennedy estate in Palm Beach, hoping the sunny weather and familiar surroundings would help him heal, but it was no use. His situation did not improve, and he sunk into a deep depression. He underwent another operation and again was in critical condition. "It was the first time I really prayed," Jackie later said. A week later, however, his condition began to improve, and on March 1, 1955, he walked for the first time without the aid of crutches.

Jack was left with an eight-inch scar on his back. "He had a hole in his back big enough for me to put my fist in it up to my wrist," said his political aide Dave Powers. It was covered by bandages that had to be changed every four hours. Jackie changed them and applied antibiotic jelly to the wound. Jack soon became much healthier but still experienced shooting

◆ PROFILES IN COURAGE ◆

While Jack was in the hospital, recovering from his back injury, Jackie encouraged him to read and write to take his mind off the pain. Jack decided he would start a book, profiling political figures who had taken stands on controversial issues.

With Jackie's help, he compiled research while in the hospital. She also found a publisher for the book—Cass Canfield, Lee's father-in-law, who worked at Harper & Brothers. Jack was given a small advance of $6,000. Published in 1956, *Profiles in Courage* got glowing reviews, hit the best-seller list, and won the Pulitzer Prize for biography.

In the acknowledgments, he thanks Jackie. "This book would not have been possible without the encouragement, assistance, and criticisms offered from the very beginning by my wife, Jacqueline, whose help during all the days of my convalescence, I cannot adequately acknowledge."

But there were those he did not acknowledge. Kennedy's young assistant, Ted Sorensen, had written major sections of the book. A former history professor of Jackie's, Jules Davids, along with Arthur Schlesinger, Jr., James MacGregor Burns, Allan Nevins, and Arthur Holcombe had also helped.

Nor was the book's success merely based on its merit. Joe Kennedy pressured his journalist friends to give the book good reviews, spent more than $100,000 on advertising, and arranged for associates to buy up the book so it would make it to the best-seller list. *Profiles in Courage* had not been nominated for a Pulitzer, but Joe Kennedy got his friend Arthur Krock to lobby for it. According to biographer Chris Anderson, the board reversed the jury's decision at Krock's request and awarded Kennedy the Pulitzer.

On December 7, 1957, on Mike Wallace's ABC show, columnist Drew Pearson charged that it was a national scandal that Kennedy won the Pulitzer for a book he had not written. Furious, Joe Kennedy wanted to sue. Instead, his lawyer, Clark Clifford, went with Jack to ABC headquarters with Jack's notes. ABC offered a retraction.

Harper editor Evan W. Thomas said, "If Jack didn't write *Profiles in Courage*, he nevertheless knew the book's contents backward and forward.."

"I think Jack supervised all of it," said George Smathers, "but how much of it he actually wrote, I would probably say very little. He was physically not able to do much writing."

pain down his lower back and left leg. He started taking Novocain as well as the cortisone shots he was already taking because of his Addison's disease.

During Jack's stay in the hospital, he conveniently missed a historic and defining vote in Congress. In December 1954 the Senate voted to censure Senator Joseph R. McCarthy, who had orchestrated the notorious witchhunt to criminalize all those Americans suspected of Communist activity. McCarthy was friendly with Joe Kennedy, who had contributed big money to his campaign. Joe didn't want his son to vote against him. Jack absorbed his father's advice and did not vote at all.

❖ ❖ ❖

"When's Inauguration Day?"

By July 1955 Jack was well enough to resume most of his normal activities. Jackie accompanied him on a seven-week congressional trip to Europe, where they met with Pope Pius XII and French premier Georges Bidault. Jackie acted as interpreter for the meeting with Bidault, who gushed over the senator's beautiful, well-educated wife—a first inkling for Jack of what a valuable asset Jackie might be to his political career.

It was on the same trip that Jack and Jackie were invited on board Aristotle Onassis's yacht, the *Christina*, moored off the Côte d'Azur for a party in honor of Sir Winston Churchill. Jack trailed Churchill all evening long, hoping to get an opportunity to talk to him, but Churchill ignored him, preferring to talk to Jackie. The snub could well have been intentional—Churchill disapproved of Joe Kennedy's isolationist beliefs. Jack pouted afterward, questioning why he had been shunned. Jackie pointed to his white dinner jacket and said, "Maybe he thought you were the waiter."

By the time the couple returned from their working vacation, Jackie was pregnant. With a child on the way, Jackie finally got a permanent home that could accommodate a family. On October 15, 1955, Jack and Jackie purchased Hickory Hill, a $125,000 estate in McLean, Virginia, complete with stables and a swimming pool. But Jackie's delight over owning a home ended abruptly when, a few days after moving in, she suffered a miscarriage. At fewer than three months of pregnancy, miscarriages were not uncommon; only the immediate family knew of Jackie's loss. Still, she was disheartened. Besides her own desire to have children, Jackie also felt a baby might curb Jack's philandering and cement their relationship. It was no surprise, then, that by early 1956 she was pregnant again.

Jack, on the other hand, was still concentrating more on the political scene than on starting a family. The Democratic National Convention was coming up in August, and it was a certainty that Adlai Stevenson, who had lost to Eisenhower in 1952, was once again going to secure the Democratic nomination. It was, however, unclear who his running mate would be. Although Jack openly declared that he wasn't interested in the vice-presidential spot, his operatives were maneuvering behind the scenes, trying to make it happen. By descending into this political arena, Jack was contradicting his father's wishes. Joe didn't want him to be on the ticket, because he didn't think Stevenson would win the general election; and worried furthermore that if Stevenson had him as a running mate, the loss would be blamed on Kennedy's Catholicism.

Eleanor Roosevelt was another who didn't want Stevenson to choose Jack, but she had a different reason. She was angry at Jack Kennedy for not speaking out against Joe McCarthy and publicly announced her opposition, saying that the Democratic Party should definitely not nominate "someone who understands what courage is and admires it, but has not quite the independence to have it."

In the midst of these political machinations, Jackie was devoting herself to decorating Hickory Hill. She took care to have it designed so Jack, with his back problems, wouldn't have trouble reaching anything. She also paid great attention to decorating the nursery. But when she was eight months pregnant Jack urged her to accompany him to Chicago for the convention. He felt it would be politically helpful, and although no doubt taken aback by Jack's total absorption in the convention and lack of concern about the expected baby, Jackie complied.

The convention turned out to be unexpectedly significant for Kennedy. Stevenson decided to throw the vice-presidential nomination out to the floor, which meant that Jack had a real chance of winning. He lost on the third ballot but did better than anyone had predicted. Although he emerged in a stronger position, Jack was understandably disappointed to lose the nomination. Jackie had never really been so closely involved in the political process before, and at one point the pressure got to her and she began weeping. It didn't help that her husband was less than attentive. Later she would claim that Jack was so caught up in the political drama that he never once spoke to her through the days of the convention.

On August 16, 1956, Jackie and Jack appeared on a national NBC television show called "Outlook." Edited out of the show was a revealing exchange between host Chet Huntley and Jackie. Hunt asked, "You're pretty much in love [with your husband], aren't you?" "Oh no," she said in her singsong voice. She then stared directly into the camera, as if she hadn't said anything wrong. Finally she murmured apologetically, "I said no, didn't I?" The interviewer, relieved to hear that her answer was a mistake, asked her again whether she was in love with her husband. This time she replied, "I suppose so."

If Jackie had already built a certain amount of resentment toward her politically ambitious, philandering husband, it was only exacerbated when Jack decided to visit his father, who was vacationing in France, to discuss the events of the convention rather than return home to Virginia with his pregnant wife. Adding to the insult, after Jack visited with his father, he scheduled a cruise with his brother Teddy and some "friends." Jackie begged him not to go. Perhaps she was aware that he would not be without female companionship. Exhausted and upset, she went to stay with her mother at Hammersmith Farm, while Jack went off to Europe.

Apparently the accumulated strain was too much. On August 23, 1956, one month before the baby was due, Jackie developed cramps so severe that she fell to the floor of her bedroom, screaming for help. She was hemorrhaging and was quickly rushed to Newport Hospital, where she underwent a premature emergency Cesarean. It was unsuccessful: The baby, a girl, was stillborn. Jackie was in critical condition after the operation, and needed several blood transfusions. A priest came to the hospital so he could administer last rites should she not pull through. Bobby Kennedy, not Jack, who was there at her bedside to tell her what had happened to the baby—whom Jackie had planned to call Arabella—and to comfort her when she heard the news. Bobby also made the necessary burial arrangements.

Meanwhile, Jack was still on his cruise, oblivious to what had happened at home. If he'd managed to get a *Washington Post* he would have seen the headline: "SENATOR KENNEDY ON MEDITERRANEAN CRUISE UNAWARE THAT HIS WIFE HAS LOST BABY." But friends weren't able to contact Jack until three days later, when the boat pulled into Genoa. Jack's reaction to the news was notably unfeeling. He said he didn't see the point of coming home, since the miscarriage had already occurred. Smathers, who was aboard the ship, set him straight, telling him he'd never be able to run for president if he didn't return. Jack packed his bags and left immediately.

Jackie, however, probably sensed that this was a PR exercise, and couldn't be so easily mollified. Outraged by Jack's total disregard for her, she also blamed him for the loss of the child and refused to return to Hickory Hill. In contrast, Jack's sisters blamed Jackie, suggesting that perhaps her aristocratic background had made her too delicate for childbirth. Jack and Jackie sold Hickory Hill, with its beautifully decorated nursery, to Bobby and Ethel. There was a particularly painful sting to this real-estate transaction since Ethel, the other Kennedy daughter-in-law, gave birth to her fifth child a couple of weeks after Jackie's Cesarean. Jackie once snidely called Ethel the "baby-making machine—wind her up and she becomes pregnant."

The couple temporarily rented another house in Georgetown, at 2808 P Street, but the tension between them grew, and they spent little time together there. For the most part, Jackie stayed in Newport with her mother, taking frequent trips to visit her sister, Lee, in New York. Jack threw himself into his work in Washington. None of this went unnoticed, and rumors quickly spread that the couple was contemplating a divorce. *Time* magazine ran a story saying that Joe Kennedy had offered his daughter-in-law $1 million to stay with his son. Although this story was flatly denied by the family, it was certainly true that Joe Kennedy knew that divorce would be political suicide for a presidential hopeful. He may never have actually offered Jackie money, but he certainly made it clear to her that there were financial advantages to remaining a member of the family. Ultimately the episode strengthened Jackie's hand with the Kennedys. She began to act as she pleased rather than as they wanted, and no longer participated in as many of the family activities as before.

One reason Jackie had to be placated was because her husband's bid for the presidency was going to come sooner rather than later. In the fall of 1956, at a Thanksgiving dinner in Hyannis Port, Joe and Jack retreated to discuss whether he should make a run for the White House in the next election, and decided the time was right.

In spring 1957, Jack and Jackie bought a home in Georgetown, at 3307 N Street NW. Jackie was once again pregnant, but this time she vowed that she wouldn't allow her husband's political plans to interfere with her pregnancy. If Jack had campaigning to do, he could do it himself. She refused to be subjected to any stress. Instead she would focus on taking care of herself and her new house.

Despite her resolve, the months that Jackie was pregnant were not without difficulties. Her father, who had never recovered from his alcoholism, had sold his seat on the New York Stock Exchange and become quite reclusive. Jackie, involved in her new life, rarely visited him anymore. He became furious when he learned of her most recent pregnancy from the *New York Times* instead of hearing it from his daughter. Still feeling insecure about his lack of financial success, he accused her of never calling or visiting, because with a fabulously wealthy father-in-law she didn't need him anymore. Soon after this

JACKIE AS CAMPAIGNER

JACKIE CAMPAIGNING WITH JOHN F. KENNEDY.

Jack used to joke that when it came to electoral appeal, his wife "had a little too much status and not enough quo." It was, in fact, a serious concern. "I thought she would come across as phony to West Virginians, as being too social," said Charlie Peters, a 1960 campaign organizer. "She wasn't going to discuss baking hams with them. She was kind of snobby and concerned with things like fashion and style to an undue extent to a West Virginian. We were planning on making poverty an issue. As it turned out, I was dead wrong. She

came and she conquered. They loved her."

Certainly Jackie was not the textbook ideal of a candidate's wife. She had a wry sense of humor that could be easily misunderstood or misconstrued by the press. And she was irreverent about politics. Once she interrupted Joe and Bobby in the midst of a heated discussion about how to solve the problem of air pollution. "I have a solution," Jackie deadpanned. "Call out the Air Force and let them spray congested urban areas with Chanel No. 5." When asked by a party official where she thought the Democratic National Convention should be held, she replied "Acapulco." When Jack's Catholicism became an issue in the election, Jackie said goodhumoredly, "I think it's so unfair of people to be against Jack because he's a Catholic. He's such a poor Catholic. Now, if it were Bobby, I could understand."

After his famous Checkers speech in 1952, Richard Nixon had turned his wife Pat's modest "Republican cloth coat" into a symbol for politicians with middle-class values. The Kennedys were far from middle class, of course, and Jack's advisers worried that Jackie's expensive tastes would alienate voters and become an issue in the press. They were right. When one newspaper charged that she spent $30,000 a year on Paris fashions, Jackie responded, "I couldn't possibly spend that much unless I wore sable underwear." Jack was furious. "Good Christ!" he said. "That's the last interview that woman will give until after the election."

Part of the problem was simply that Jackie disliked politics. Even though she had married a congressman, she looked down on politicians as bourgeois and hypocritical. She resented having to hide the fact that she smoked. She had to keep Caroline's nanny, Maude Shaw, out of the public eye and pretend that she raised her daughter herself.

For the most part, Jackie was able to hide how she really felt about politics. When Jackie was campaigning with Jack in Kenosha, Wisconsin, she went to a local supermarket and asked to use the loudspeaker. "Just keep on with your shopping while I tell you about my husband, John F. Kennedy," she announced to the store full of housewives. She described his career in politics, as well as his record in the military, and ended with a simple request: "Please vote for him."

At campaign rallies she would tell the crowds that her daughter's first few words were "Good-bye," "New Hampshire," "Wisconsin," and "West Virginia." Jackie joked that she was "sorry so few states have primaries, or we would have a daughter with the greatest vocabulary of any two year old in the country." The young political wife also turned her highbrow education to her husband's advantage by using her French and Italian in ethnic precincts.

Despite her growing skill at campaigning, Jackie never overcame her discomfort with, and disdain for, the process. According to Ben Bradlee, when Jackie was out campaigning with Jack she was able "to pull some invisible shade down across her face, and cut out spiritually. She was physically present but intellectually long gone."

Sometimes her true sentiments would reveal themselves unexpectedly. Wayne Koestenbaum describes such a moment in his book *Jackie Under My Skin*. "In the 'At Home with the Kennedys' TV spot, in which Rose and Jackie chat together on the couch, Rose notes how lucky Jack was to find a wife who loved campaigning; but when Jackie says that she feels like she's shaken every hand in Massachusetts, her singsong yet expressionless voice . . . turns the line to parody, and we realize, in retrospect, that Jackie did *not* enjoy campaigning. . . ."

argument, on July 27, 1957, the eve of Jackie's twenty-eighth birthday, Black Jack, then sixty-six years old, was admitted to New York's Lenox Hill Hospital. Five days later he lapsed into a coma, and Jackie was told for the first time that her father had long been suffering from liver cancer. She raced to his bedside, but he was dead before she arrived. The nurses told her that Black Jack's last word was "Jackie." Whatever anger he felt about his daughter's neglect was not reflected in his will. Jackie and Lee each received $80,000.

Jackie was five months pregnant when her father was buried in East Hampton. There was fear that the strain of his death might once again endanger her pregnancy. But those fears were put to rest when, on November 27, Jackie gave birth to a healthy baby girl at Cornell University Medical Center. She weighed seven pounds, two ounces, and they called her Caroline. Jack, who had all along seemed so indifferent about the baby, was ecstatic.

A British nanny, Maude Shaw, moved into their new Georgetown home to help take care of the new baby. On the surface Jackie seemed to have many of the things she yearned for: a child, a home, and financial security. Nevertheless, she was far from content and threw herself into redecorating her new home with near-maniacal zeal. She rearranged their belongings so frequently that even Jack, who was oblivious to most domestic details, became irritated. "Dammit, Jackie, why is it that the rooms in this house are never completely livable all at the same time?" She began to spend outrageous amounts of money on clothes and suffered extreme mood swings.

Caroline's birth did not interfere with Jack's single-minded focus on his career. His Senate reelection campaign was coming up, and although it was never in doubt that he would win, there was some concern about the magnitude of the victory.

His advisers believed that if he could win by five hundred thousand votes, he'd have enough momentum to win his party's nomination for the presidency. Knowing that nothing warmed the heart of the electorate like an adorable child with a doting father, Jack agreed to let various publications photograph his daughter. At first Jackie was upset, but eventually she gave in. With Caroline's help, Jack won reelection handily, with more than the margin he needed to justify a bid for the presidency. He spent much of 1959 laying the groundwork, and in January 1960 formally declared his candidacy for the nation's highest office.

First, there were six other Democratic candidates to beat during the primaries. Despite her disdain for politics, Jackie campaigned with her husband for much of this time, showing the same resolve she demonstrated at his bedside when he was near death. Nevertheless, some Kennedy advisers thought she might be a liability: Would the electorate warm to a fashionable political wife who was so clearly identifiable with high society? In the end, it was not an issue. At the convention, Jack secured 761 delegate votes and won the Democratic nomination, choosing Texas senator Lyndon Johnson as his running mate.

Jackie did not attend the Los Angeles convention; she was pregnant again and felt she should take it easy. Jack didn't mind that his wife remained at home, but it was probably less out of concern for her health than for more selfish reasons. His extramarital affairs were becoming dangerously brazen. At a victory party that evening at the house of his brother-in-law Peter Lawford, the guests, who included such celebrities as Angie Dickinson and Marilyn Monroe, went skinny-dipping in the outdoor pool. The party got so out of hand that the police turned up, backing down only when they realized one of the revelers was the new Democratic nominee.

Jackie with her daughter, Caroline, in Hyannis Port, 1960.

Jack now had to face a new opponent: Republican Richard Nixon. Jackie was unable to campaign as vigorously during the general election because of her pregnancy, and professed regret that she wasn't able to help. "I suppose I won't be able to play much part in the campaign," she told reporters, "but I'll do what I can. I feel I should be with Jack when he's engaged in such a struggle, and if it weren't for the baby, I'd campaign even more vigorously than Mrs. Nixon."

As it turned out, the election was decided by just a few votes: Kennedy won the popular vote by the narrowest of margins, collecting just 118,550 more votes than his opponent. While the Kennedy clan celebrated by playing a game of touch football, Jackie suddenly realized the enormity of what lay ahead of her and strolled the beach, alone, crying. At thirty-one years of age, she would be among the youngest First Ladies in American history. She must have felt woefully unprepared. When asked by reporters if the baby was due before or after Inauguration Day, Jackie replied, "When's Inauguration Day?"

1961

CHAPTER FIVE

FIRST LADY

———◆———

The months leading up to the inauguration were hectic. The Kennedys' Georgetown home was bustling nearly nonstop with political advisers. "It was so crowded that I could be in the bathroom, in the tub," Jackie later said, "and then find [Jack's press secretary] Pierre Salinger was holding a press conference in my bedroom." When he wasn't working at home, Jack was either at the family's Palm Beach estate, seeking guidance from his father, or in Texas, consulting with his vice president–elect, Lyndon Johnson. Jackie was no less preoccupied. Although already eight months pregnant when Jack won the election, she had to begin selecting members of her own staff right away as well as start thinking about what cause she might get involved in as First Lady, and she had to oversee and orchestrate her family's move to the White House. One of her staffing decisions, however, was made for her: Jack hired Pamela Turnure, a receptionist in his Senate office with whom he was rumored to be having an affair, to be Jackie's press secretary. This was an altogether new post: No previous First Lady had had enough media requests to warrant a press secretary. Although Turnure had no experience dealing with the media, Jackie appeared enthusiastic about the choice and sent her new employee a note welcoming her.

To add to this pressure, Jackie also had a tight deadline to meet, since she had agreed to collaborate with journalist and longtime family friend Mary Van Rensselaer Thayer on a book about her life for Doubleday. The book, which would be titled *Jacqueline Bouvier Kennedy*, had already attracted intense media attention long before it had even been completed. *Ladies' Home Journal* paid $150,000 for first serial rights—a huge sum, even by today's standards, for a magazine excerpt. Since Jackie was such a private person, one might assume that writing an autobiography was anathema to her. But she was also concerned about her public image, and no doubt understood that the project presented an opportunity to admit that some of the "aristocratic" elements in her family tree were more fictional than factual, thereby preempting scandal-seeking journalists. She took the assignment very seriously and became deeply involved in the collaboration, staying up late most nights to write out stories about her childhood.

Given Jackie's history of difficult pregnancies, this schedule—and increasingly intense public scrutiny—soon proved taxing. The president-elect, however, had even more pressing matters to worry about and was less than sympathetic to his wife's complaints. "Oh, for God's sake, Jackie," he said. "All you have to worry about is your inaugural gown." Even if that had been true, however, it would have been enough to make Jackie anxious. She was well aware that Bess Truman and Mamie Eisenhower had left the public starved for a stylish First

Lady, and that as an unusually young and attractive wife of a president, a great deal was expected of her.

Three weeks before Jackie was due to give birth, she and Jack spent Thanksgiving together in their home. After the holiday dinner, however, Jack flew to Palm Beach for a strategy session with Joe. Jackie asked her husband not to go, believing it was too close to their delivery date, but Jack went anyway. Only an hour after he boarded his plane, the *Caroline*, Maude Shaw, the family nanny, heard Jackie scream out in pain. She was hemorrhaging. Jackie was rushed to the hospital for an emergency Cesarean. Jack, still on the plane when he heard that his wife had gone into labor, feared that the past was repeating itself and that they might again lose a child.

This time the baby survived. Jack, still airborne when he learned that Jackie had given birth to a healthy boy, took a bow when Pierre Salinger made a congratulatory announcement over the aircraft's intercom. Despite his safe arrival on November 26, 1960, however, John, Jr. was small—six pounds, three ounces—and weak enough that the doctors decided he had to be placed in an incubator.

While still in the hospital, Jackie began to concentrate more closely on her inaugural wardrobe, and it was there that she settled on Oleg Cassini to be her designer. As well as being an American, a positive for the First Lady who had been criticized during the campaign for her predilections for Parisian designers, Cassini had indirect connections to Jackie—his brother was the journalist who had named her Debutante of the Year—and direct connections to the Kennedys: He dined with Joe once a week at La Caravelle in New York, designed clothes for Rose, and had contributed to Jack's campaign. If these qualifications weren't enough, no doubt Joe Kennedy's pledge to foot the clothing bill if Cassini was chosen influenced Jackie's decision.

"I talked to her like a movie star," Cassini later said, and told her she needed a story, a scenario as First Lady. Although Jackie was not accustomed to thinking of herself as a movie star, she probably knew that she required what Cassini, a former Hollywood costume designer, called "a story." If she didn't stage-manage her own public persona, the press would create one for her—a most unattractive prospect to such an image-conscious woman. A public persona would also provide a shield of sorts for her inner life. If she stood for something definite and concrete in the popular imagination, there might be less curiosity about her private life. People would think they knew her, but she would still be able to control just how much they really did know.

Not surprisingly, she took a very active role in planning her wardrobe as First Lady. "Make sure no one has exactly the same dress I do," she instructed Cassini. "I want all mine to be original and no fat little women hopping around in the same dress." She explained how afraid she was that she would develop a reputation for being frivolous. "I refuse to have Jack's administration plagued by fashion stories of a sensational nature," she announced, adding that she didn't want to be considered "the Marie Antoinette or Josephine of the 1960s." Believing the press was out to get her, she wrote Cassini, "Protect me—as I seem so mercilessly exposed and don't know how to cope with it (I read tonight I dye my hair because it is mousy gray)." She told him that absolutely no information about her wardrobe should be made public without her consent. After all, she concluded, "there may just be a few things we won't tell them about."

When Jackie left the hospital, she still felt quite weak from the difficult delivery, but had to embark immediately on her new official duties. First was a tour of the White House, which

First Lady Mamie Eisenhower had offered to conduct personally. Jackie wanted to cancel, but Jack insisted she keep the
appointment; as a precaution, her doctor called the White
House to explain Jackie's condition and ensure that there would
be a wheelchair waiting for her. Mrs. Eisenhower, however,
thought it would be particularly humiliating for the outgoing
First Lady to push her successor around the White House. So
rather than have the wheelchair waiting out in the open for
Jackie, it was kept in a closet, to be brought out only if she
requested it. But Jackie was so intimidated by Mrs. Eisenhower
that she never asked for the wheelchair. After the two-hour
tour, Jackie left the White House physically exhausted—and
distinctly unimpressed by her new home.

She complained to Letitia "Tish" Baldrige, her longtime
friend and newly hired social secretary, that the First
Residence looked like a "hotel that had been decorated by a
wholesale furniture store during a January clearance." All
First Ladies were expected to have special projects, and one of
hers would be the restoration of the White House. To prepare,
she immediately began studying blueprints and photographs
of the rooms and the grounds.

Jackie had deeper worries about living in the White House
than how she would redecorate it. One was the press: How
could she protect herself from its invasive attentions after she
moved into what was, in effect, a publicly funded fishbowl?
Before the election, the media had focused mainly on her
charismatic husband, but now journalists were also hounding
the future First Lady. She disliked reporters intensely and
reacted poorly to them. She was incensed when a photographer
leaped out of a hospital closet and began snapping pictures
when she went to visit John, Jr. in the incubator room. She complained when the *Washington Post* reported that she had hem-

orrhaged, because she believed that the term wasn't dignified enough to apply to the First Lady.

Jackie's second concern was her family's physical safety. She worried constantly about the dangers of public life, particularly after the family's December stay at the estate in Palm Beach. When one Richard Pavlick was arrested for drunk driving, he told the police that he had armed his car with seven sticks of dynamite and had been ready to ram Jack's car as Jack was leaving for Mass until he saw Jackie and the children come out to kiss him good-bye. He didn't want to harm anyone but Jack, Pavlick said, so he decided to abort the plan for the time being—but kill the president-elect at a later date. Naturally, Jackie was unnerved by the incident. "We're nothing but sitting ducks in a shooting gallery," she exclaimed.

On January 19, 1961, the day before the swearing-in ceremony, a snowstorm paralyzed Washington; there were traffic jams everywhere. The first inaugural event took place that evening at Constitution Hall: a gala concert organized by Kennedy friend Frank Sinatra and Jack's brother-in-law Peter Lawford. Jackie wore a simple white satin gown designed by Cassini. Jack loved it so much that he paid her a rare compliment. On their way to the concert, after dining at the home of *Washington Post* owner Philip Graham and his wife, Katharine, Jack requested that the light in the limousine be turned on so the crowds lining the snow-covered streets could see Jackie.

The gala featured a star-studded cast: Ella Fitzgerald, Bette Davis, Leonard Bernstein, Shirley MacLaine, and Tony Curtis. Mahalia Jackson performed a rendition of "The Star-Spangled Banner" and Frank Sinatra sang his hit "That Old Black Magic," substituting the word "Jack" for "Black." Afterward Jackie, still not fully recovered from childbirth, went home, but Jack continued the celebrations at a party thrown by his father, returning only a few hours before he had to get ready for the next day's events.

By morning, several inches of snow had accumulated, and though the sun was shining brightly, it was bitterly cold. Jack was nervous, not least because Jackie was running late, a habit he complained about constantly. Clad in a Cassini-designed, fawn-colored wool coat with a sable-trimmed collar, she added her own sable muff to keep her hands warm. The outfit had a schoolgirlish charm, but what made the biggest fashion impression that day was her matching pillbox hat designed by Halston. Inauguration Day was very windy, and at one point Jackie reached up to secure her hat and by accident put a slight dent in it. But the public didn't realize it was unintentional; they thought the pillbox was designed that way. Almost immediately, women started putting dents in their own hats, and designers scrambled to manufacture predented ones. As would be true throughout her life, the smallest details of Jackie's wardrobe were carefully studied and widely imitated. Even items she chose for their practicality, such as her fake pearls or oversized sunglasses, would almost instantly attain status as high-style classics simply because they had her seal of approval.

The ceremony began at 11:40 A.M., with Chief Justice Earl Warren administering the oath of office, Cardinal Cushing delivering the invocation, and Marian Anderson singing the National Anthem. The eighty-six-year-old poet Robert Frost had written a poem for the occasion, but the sunlight was so blinding that he was unable to read his own words. Instead, he recited a poem he knew by heart. At 12:51 P.M. the second-youngest U.S. president in history was officially sworn in, and began delivering his inaugural address, which included the famous lines, "Ask not what your country can do for you. Ask what you can do for your country."

After the swearing-in, Jackie, rarely one for public displays of affection, stroked her husband's cheek and quietly said, "You were wonderful." She later explained: "There was so much I wanted to say. But I could scarcely embrace him in front of all those people."

There were several luncheons that afternoon, including a particularly strained affair with the Bouvier, Auchincloss, Lee, and Kennedy relatives, where the four clans kept to themselves and made little effort to mingle. After lunch, the parade began marching up Pennsylvania Avenue, but after a short distance Jackie excused herself early and headed to her new home at 1600 Pennsylvania Avenue, to rest for the five gala balls she was expected to attend that evening.

Her New York hairdresser Kenneth and her Palm Beach masseuse were on hand to help her prepare for that evening. Jackie wore a white silk crepe gown with a bodice embroidered in silver thread that had been made by Bergdorf Goodman before she chose Cassini as her personal designer. To ward off the chill she also donned a dramatic, sweeping cape and long white opera gloves.

Jack Kennedy thrived on the fundamentals of politics and drew energy from adoring crowds. "I don't know a better way to spend an evening," Kennedy told the audience at one of the galas. "You looking at us, and we looking at you." Jackie's reaction that night reflected a different attitude toward the interaction between a leader and the led. "Just a bunch of people standing around like mesmerized cattle," she said. At midnight, after attending the balls at the Mayflower Hotel, the Statler Hilton, and the Armory, Jackie was exhausted and had to return home. Jack went on without her to the other two balls and then attended a party at the home of journalist Joe Alsop.

Jackie with John, Jr.

Behind the glittering scenes of the inauguration, family politics were being played out, according to Jackie's stepbrother Jamie Auchincloss. He recalls that amid all the distractions Jackie was dealing with as First Lady, she hadn't been meeting her deadlines for the book she was writing with Mary Van Rennselaer Thayer. It's unclear whether she lost interest, became too busy, or decided that the book wasn't a good idea after all. Whatever the case, Janet Auchincloss, without permission, recounted some of her daughter's childhood stories to Thayer. She believed she was helping her daughter out. "My mother just chatted away," recalls Jamie Auchincloss. When the stories appeared in *Ladies' Home Journal*, Jackie was stunned. She didn't think that any story could be printed without her cooperation. "She didn't realize that my mother was the secret source," says Jamie. When Jackie found out, she was angry and determined to retaliate.

"My parents were supposed to be sent really fine tickets to the inauguration—you know, the best VIP tickets you could have as the mother- and father-in-law to the president of the United States," Jamie explains. Instead, Jackie switched her parents' tickets with those of Jamie and his sister, Janet. "I sat next to Eleanor Roosevelt, who was sitting next to Adlai Stevenson, and my parents sat at the very top of the inaugural stand. All they could see was the very back of Jack's head."

Apparently this mixed-up seating arrangement went on all day, until Kennedy himself realized at one of the evening galas that he hadn't seen his wife's parents. One of the better-known photographs from that day shows the new president on his feet, pointing out and up in the distance, as if he were urging the country to look with him toward the New Frontier of the future. But according to Auchincloss, Kennedy was actually pointing to his parents-in-law; he finally spied them perched in seats so distant they might as well have been in the rafters. "Jackie was playing completely dumb about it," Auchincloss recalled.

❦ ❦ ❦

"I mean kings and queens—that's fine"

Kennedy's years in the White House were marked by crises abroad and turmoil at home. The young president had hardly settled into office before he presided over the Bay of Pigs fiasco. The Soviets heightened Cold War tensions by building the Berlin Wall and then brought the world to the brink of nuclear holocaust in the Cuban Missile Crisis. At home, Kennedy had to face down the nation's big steel companies over price increases and contend with civil rights distubances in the South.

While her husband was dealing with considerable burdens, Jackie for the most part remained uninterested. Never politically inclined, Jackie could be quite irreverent about her status, and liked to joke that "First Lady" sounded like the name of a racehorse. Their Secret Service names were lighthearted: Jack was "Lancer," she was "Lace," and Caroline and John, Jr. were "Lyric" and "Lark," respectively. Unlike some other First Ladies, most notably Eleanor Roosevelt, Jackie did not play an active role in any policy decisions. The young woman who said her main goal was "not to be a housewife" had undergone what appeared to be a complete metamorphosis. Although she lived in the White House, she was, in fact, not unlike many other women in the 1950s: Her main goals were to raise her children and provide diversions for her husband. Because she shared their aims, other women could identify with her; because she conducted herself with such élan, they also emulated her. Jackie was the rarest of political creatures: ordinary enough to be nonthreatening but elevated enough to inspire admiration.

Her brief forays into the political arena seemed motivated more by her emotional response to a particular issue than by any driving interest in public policy. Because she had been shocked during the campaign by the poverty in West Virginia, while in the White House she insisted on using glassware from that state rather than the finer Steuben glasses that were offered to them. If it would help the state's economy, she declared, "I would practically break all the glasses and order new ones each week." She even encouraged the manufacturer to publicize her endorsement.

Within the family, her disinterest in politics was so well known that Bobby once fed her a bogus policy question so she could play a joke on her husband. Does "confirming Albert Breeson to membership on the National Labor Relations Board," she asked the president, "[have] the effect of wrecking the Bonwit Teller clause of the National Labor Relations Act?" Kennedy convulsed with laughter.

Jackie told the chief of protocol, Angier Biddle Duke, that she had no intention of attending all the official events to which she was invited. "I mean kings and queens—that's fine. But all those banana-republic presidents—forget it. Can't we work out a way to give them the PBO?" she asked, referring, as she often did, to the "polite brush-off." "Can't we give them to Lady Bird to handle?" Jackie wasn't joking.

Although she had decided that her goal as First Lady would be to raise the level of culture and sophistication of the American capital, Jackie firmly believed that her most important White House project was raising her family. The First Lady she most admired and hoped to emulate was Bess Truman, who had made her husband's and daughter's welfare her top priority. "If you bungle raising your children," Jackie once said, "I don't think whatever else you do matters very much." Although her mornings were spent taking care of administration business and exercising—she regularly took hour-long walks around the grounds—her afternoons were devoted to her children. She refused requests to take on more official tasks. "If I were to add political duties," she explained, "I would have practically no time with my children."

Spending time with her husband was also crucial to Jackie. While the children napped in the afternoon, the couple spent several hours alone. This was an unshakable part of Jackie's daily schedule, according to J. B. West, the chief White House usher. "Mrs. Kennedy dropped everything, no matter how important, to join her husband," he reported. "If she had visitors in tow, they would be left for me to entertain." But Jackie never viewed her time with Jack in terms of routine. Although she dressed casually during the day, she made a point of dressing up for her husband in the evenings, whether they were attending a state dinner or dining alone.

"It must be restored. . . ."

The White House was a cold, impersonal place for a young family, and one of Jackie's early tasks was making the private living areas more comfortable and welcoming. She asked the New York decorator who had helped her fix up one of her Georgetown homes to assist in redecorating their new quarters. "No Mamie pink on the walls," she instructed, "except in Caroline's room." With the decorator's help, she designed a new kitchen closer to the room in which they ate so their food wouldn't get cold by the time it was brought to them. She also set up a play area outside the Oval Office, with swings, slides, and a trampoline for John, Jr. and Caroline.

But Jackie's plans for the rest of the White House were far loftier. She told her decorator that it "would be sacrilege merely to 'redecorate' it—a word I hate. It must be restored. . . ."

When the Kennedys moved in, the White House was filled with bland furnishings that were more institutional than aesthetic. She was particularly appalled that all the antiques, which were so redolent of the nation's history, had been removed. Believing the White House should reflect the leaders who had lived in it, she aimed to install one piece of furniture or art from every administration. To that end, she convened a Fine Arts Committee and a White House Historical Association, and convinced experts in art history and Americana to participate. White House legal counsel Clark Clifford explained that no public funds could be requested for this project, so Jackie solicited private donations. She also came up with the idea of publishing a White House guidebook, once the restoration was completed, to raise money for the project. *The White House: An Historic Guide* was a phenomenal success.

Jackie expended huge amounts of time and energy on the restoration, rummaging through a warehouse where old White House furniture was stored and soliciting donations from descendants of past presidents. The results were gratifying. When the restoration was completed, the White House was much improved. Even some of the grounds had been transformed, most notably the Rose Garden. Yet along the way were numerous obstacles. Although Jackie vowed that the restoration would not be partisan in any respect, the project proved to be a political minefield. According to Pierre Salinger, Jack was initially against the idea, fearing it would be perceived as frivolous, and believing that the public would rather the White House stay as it was. Other naysayers had two main objections. The first was that Jackie was straying from authenticity and relying too heavily on her own instincts and taste. (For example, she decided the Blue Room should be white with blue accents.) Second, critics charged that she was too much the Francophile, selecting anything French over American counterparts. But Jackie prevailed. She had a talent for blocking out things she preferred not to hear, whether it was a rumor about her husband's lastest extramarital fling or a criticism of her approach to redesigning the White House. "In this job, there's always going to be a flare up about something," she once said. "And you must somehow get so it doesn't upset you. I think I was always fairly good at it. I can drop down this curtain in my mind."

She managed to convert Jack to her way of thinking so much that he urged her to lead a televised tour of the White House, correctly predicting that it would help the project gain public approval. Although hesitant because she didn't think she came off very well on TV, she agreed, joining correspondent Charles Collingwood taking Americans room by room through the mansion. According to Collingwood, Jackie's assessment of her on-camera skills was accurate. "It was the first time American audiences saw her for any extended period of time," he later said, "and her breathless voice and that deer-caught-in-the-headlights look did take some getting used to." The First Lady seemed to him rattled by even the most benign unscripted comments. For instance, when they entered the Blue Room, Collingwood said to Jackie, "Oh, this has a very different feeling from the Red Room." Jackie seemed at a loss, blurting out, "Yes. It's blue."

There was one contemporary critic: writer Norman Mailer, who lambasted her wooden performance. "She walked through the program like a starlet who would never learn to act," he said, adding that the show was "silly, ill-advised, pointless, empty, dull, and obsequious to the most slavish tastes in America." Years later, even Jackie admirer and author Wayne Koestenbaum would reflect that she seemed "like a docent on drugs."

But despite her awkward television presence, "A Tour of the White House with Mrs. John F. Kennedy" was a huge success, garnering at least 56 million viewers. Many of them were moved to send donations; after the program was aired on all three networks, $2 million in small donations arrived for the project. The program was a huge hit abroad as well: Fourteen foreign nations requested rights to air it.

❖ ❖ ❖

"The Jackie Look"

Interest in the stylish, urbane young inhabitants of the White House reached fever pitch. Jackie became famous for throwing glamorous dinner parties, hosting more than sixty-five during her three years in the White House. Unlike past White House affairs, where rubber chicken and a stuffy atmosphere prevailed, Kennedy dinners were remarkable because of the Gatsbyesque attention to detail, not to mention the fine food and wines on which Jackie insisted. She replaced the long U-shaped tables traditionally used for state dinners with smaller, round ones, to promote intimate conversations. And she drew up impressive guest lists that mixed literary and artistic giants with the usual suspects: diplomats and politicians. Since one of Jackie's goals was to elevate the arts to the same sort of status they had in Europe, she broke with tradition and invited performers to entertain, a practice that continues. Jerome Robbins staged a ballet; the American Shakespeare Festival appeared. But Jackie's biggest coup was convincing Spanish cellist Pablo Casals to play. Casals, who had been living in self-imposed exile in Puerto Rico, was opposed to performing in any country that recognized Spanish dictator Francisco Franco, yet he agreed to perform at the White House for Jackie.

Shooting of "A Tour of the White House with Mrs. John F. Kennedy."

Jackie's interest in the arts went far beyond securing talent to liven up state dinners. She also believed that government funding should be increased, even for experimental arts. Jackie encouraged her husband to support legislation to create a Washington National Cultural Center (later renamed the Kennedy Center) to rival New York's Lincoln Center, and argued vigorously for the establishment of government institutions to support art and literature, a vision that was realized with the subsequent creation of the National Endowment of the Arts and the National Endowment for the Humanities. Although Jack was never known as a devotee of the arts (he favored show tunes and rock and roll music to the symphony and the opera), Jackie claimed that he "shared the conviction that the artist should be honored by society." In retrospect, given the way that writers and artists and the rest of the intelligentsia came to lionize President Kennedy and support his policies, this seems like a shrewd move on Jackie's part. Despite her characteristic reserve, she was openly passionate about the arts, and artists returned the favor. "What a joy that literacy is no longer prima facie evidence of treason," novelist John Steinbeck quipped.

Yet no matter what Jackie did to bring culture and sophistication to the White House, what the public seemed to care about most was her wardrobe. The "Jackie Look" became famous around the world. Anything she wore—Pucci pants, pillbox hats, low pumps, strapless evening dresses—was instantly copied by Seventh Avenue manufacturers. When the First Lady was pregnant, the maternity-wear designer Lane Bryant produced a knockoff line called First Lady Fashion. Across the ocean British milliners received thousands of orders for pillbox hats, and even *Mody*, a Soviet magazine in Leningrad, ran advertisements for the "Jackie Look."

As Jackie fever swept across America, she became the first First Lady to attain the status of pop culture icon. Her bouffant was all the rage at hairdressing salons across America. Fan magazines ran articles titled "How to Be Your Town's Jacqueline Kennedy," and Vaughn Meader's "First Family" records successfully spoofed Jack's Boston accent and Jackie's breathless voice. In an episode of the television series, "The Flintstones," Betty and Wilma squealed, "It's the Jackie Kennelrock Look!" when they saw a department store mannequin sporting a bouffant hairdo and pillbox hat. As Carl Sferrazza Anthony points out, in Hollywood the brainy brunette emerged as a rival to the ditzy blondes who had so long epitomized sex appeal, and on television, Mary Tyler Moore's Laura Petrie on "The Dick Van Dyke Show" was clearly modeled on the First Lady. Jackie became so popular in her own right that the president regularly included lines about her in his political addresses. In his best inspirational tone, he once told a group of visiting students that one of them might possibly return to the White House as president someday. "Or better yet," he joked, "as a president's wife."

The American public could not seem to get enough information about the First Family. Journalists were sent to cover the Kennedys in full force, and photos of the children at play in the White House and of Caroline riding her pony, Macaroni, were favorites with the press. Jackie, who had always strived to protect her children's privacy, loathed the press. Asked by a journalist what her German shepherd liked to eat, she once replied, "Reporters." Once, signaling her contempt, the renowned hostess served the female members of the press corps Kool-Aid at an afternoon tea.

Jack did not share her feelings. "You have to remember," said Ben Bradlee, "that this was the first real television presidency. The children were very photogenic. Politically, Jack must have thought—what an asset." According to photographer Jacques Lowe, JFK would encourage him to come and take pictures of the children when Jackie was out of town. "It got to be a game between the two of them, with me stuck in the middle." If it was explained that JFK had given approval for pictures to be taken of the children, Jackie would retort, "I don't give a damn. He had no right to countermand my order regarding the children." Her desire for privacy and his appetite for publicity could never be reconciled. After a photographer secretly followed Jackie to her friend Bunny

Mellon's Virginia estate and got pictures of her being thrown from a horse, she asked Jack to prevent publication, arguing that it was an egregious, unforgivable violation. He disagreed. "I'm sorry, Jackie," he said with a laugh, "but when the First Lady falls on her ass, that's news."

If America's infatuation with the new First Lady was to be expected, given her age and good looks, her star status abroad was much more of a surprise. The first indication came during the couple's first foreign trip, in 1961, to Ottawa, Canada, where Jackie wore a red suit to match the colors of the Royal Canadian Mounted Police. "Mrs. Kennedy's charm, beauty, vivacity, and grace of mind have captured our hearts," said the Speaker of the Canadian Senate. "Many Canadians searched the civil registers to see if she was a Canadian."

From there the couple flew to Paris. The typically indifferent French were out en masse to greet them—or so it seemed at first. It quickly became evident that the quarter of a million people lining the streets had actually come out to see her, not him. The crowd went wild, chanting, *"Vive Jacqui! Vive Jacqui!"* as she passed by in the motorcade. During a dinner at Versailles, Jackie was seated next to De Gaulle, who was taken with the beautiful First Lady and so impressed with her knowledge of French history and culture that he later told JFK, "I now have more confidence in your country." The press dubbed the phenomenon *"La Fièvre de Jacqueline."*

There was another observer thoroughly impressed with Jackie: her husband. Viewing her through others' eyes, it was as though he were seeing her anew. He did not begrudge her popularity, even when it eclipsed his own. At a press conference he joked, "I do not think it's altogether inappropriate to introduce myself to this audience. I am the man who accompanied Jacqueline Kennedy to Paris, and I have enjoyed it."

From Paris, they traveled to Vienna for a summit meeting with Soviet premier Nikita Khrushchev. The meeting was a disaster for the young president, and he knew it. Kennedy told journalist James Reston that the meeting was "the worst thing in my life. [Khrushchev] rolled right over me—he thinks I'm a fool—he thinks I'm weak."

Jackie was more successful. There was little question about Khrushchev's feelings for the First Lady. At a state banquet that evening, the Soviet leader demanded that he be seated next to Jackie. He boasted to the lovely young American at his side that there were more schoolteachers in the Ukraine under the Soviets than there had been under Czarist rule. Aware of his infatuation, Jackie coquettishly replied, "Oh, Mr. Chairman, don't bore me with statistics." Like De Gaulle, the Soviet leader was charmed. Over dinner Jackie discussed the Russian dogs that had been sent into space during the previous month, asking if she could have one of their puppies. A couple of months later, a puppy arrived at the White House, and the Kennedys named it Pushinka, which means "Fluffy" in Russian.

As frivolous as it may seem, the encounter served a purpose. The Soviets had recently embarrassed the United States by beating America in the race to send a manned mission into space. By reducing the highly charged space race to a conversation about puppies, Jackie helped defuse some of the tension that was contributing to the U.S.–Soviet rivalry. There was something else: "Posed next to grandmotherly Nina Khrushchev," author Wayne Koestenbaum wrote later, "Jackie seemed evidence that, if choosing between capitalism and communism were a choice between Jackie and Nina, one would be smart to pick capitalism."

Pushinka was not the only special gift sent to the White

House by a foreign leader as a tribute to Jackie. André Malraux, the French minister of culture, loaned the most famous painting in the world, Da Vinci's *Mona Lisa*, to the United States in January 1963. The painting wasn't loaned to the government, however. It instead was a personal loan to the First Lady herself.

Jackie's travels abroad were so successful that when she had finished restoring the White House, Jack encouraged her to take trips by herself. Thus in March 1962, America's first Catholic First Lady flew to Rome for an audience with the pope, later followed by a trip to India.

In the summer of 1962, Jackie took Caroline on a trip to Ravello, a village on Italy's Amalfi coast where Lee and her new husband, Stas Radziwill, had rented a villa. Jackie stayed much longer than the expected two weeks, water-skiing and sunbathing, causing murmurs in the press about her excessive cosmopolitanism. "Jacqueline Kennedy had originally planned to stay at Ravello for two weeks," *Time* magazine reported. "But the two became three, and now they have stretched into four. She was having such a wonderful time that it almost seemed she might yet declare herself a permanent resident." Rumors began to circulate that one reason for Jackie's lengthy stay was another houseguest: Gianni Agnelli, Fiat chairman and heir to the company's fortune. When paparazzi photographs appeared of the two swimming together and dancing barefoot on the deck of his eighty-two-foot yacht, JFK cabled his wife: "A LITTLE MORE CAROLINE AND LESS AGNELLI." Jackie reacted by going scuba diving with Agnelli the following day.

Jackie had become so popular that Jack had begun to find her far more appealing. Aware of this, Jackie may have decided to torment him with extramarital dalliances, just as he had to her. Jackie's decision to prolong her visit to Ravello may have had as much to do with Marilyn Monroe, whose death by overdose had just occurred, as it did with Agnelli. Because she knew Jack had been having an affair with Monroe, Jackie may have wanted to be as far away from the White House as possible in the aftermath of her death.

Despite evidence of their affairs, Tish Baldrige claims Jack and Jackie had a very tender relationship and shared an irreverent sensibility about the world they found themselves in. "She used to leave funny little notes all over the White House to cheer him up," Baldrige recounts. "He'd read one of these little notes and burst out laughing." Jackie would also amuse him by mimicking guests after they left. "Jackie could be just hilarious," said Baldrige. "The way she imitated people's accents, their mannerisms—it was uncannily accurate. These were some of the most respected, revered people in the world, and the imitations she did once they left the room were just withering."

Several events early in Jack's presidency drew him even closer to his wife. On December 19, 1961, Joe Kennedy suffered a massive stroke, leaving him paralyzed on his right side and unable to speak. Jack, who had been so reliant on his father, now turned more often to his wife.

October 1962 brought the Cuban Missile Crisis, the closest the world has ever come to a war between two nuclear powers. Before Kennedy addressed the nation about the severity of the situation, he called Jackie, who was vacationing at Glen Ora on Cape Cod, and asked her to return to Washington to be with him, which she did. Jack's friend Chuck Spalding found the president's behavior telling. "If it was earlier in their marriage, I don't think he would have called her then," said Spalding. The Pentagon planned to evacuate the White House and send Kennedy to a fortified

◆ FIRST LADIES ◆

JACKIE AT DINNER AT JAPANESE EMBASSY.

America had never seen a First Lady like Jackie. Prior to the Kennedy administration, First Ladies tended to be more like First Mothers, matronly figures who hovered in the background and were fairly anonymous. The exceptions were First Ladies such as Eleanor Roosevelt and Edith Wilson who actively engaged in their husbands' political lives but who lacked the style to capture the popular imagination. Jackie was neither matronly nor politically active. She was above both in a way—part princess, part movie star. She brought beauty, fashion, and sophistication to a position that by and large had lacked all three in the past. She captivated the public, setting trends that would outlast her years in the White House and leaving a daunting legacy for those who followed her.

For years afterward, several of Jackie's successors attempted to fashion themselves in her image, with little success. As early as October 31, 1967, *Look* magazine had dubbed Nancy Reagan a "Republican version of Jacqueline Kennedy," noting her "same spare figure . . . same air of immaculate chic." And when Nancy entered the White House in 1981, she had every intention of having the general public reach the same conclusion. The press had already focused on Mrs. Reagan's style, much as it had with Jackie. The new First Lady put great care into selecting her inaugural gowns, choosing items that were reminiscent of Jackie's attire two decades earlier. For her husband's swearing-in ceremony, Mrs. Reagan wore a bright red oval hat that led CBS commentator Roger Mudd to draw the comparison to Jackie's pillbox hat. For the inaugural gala she had her hair styled in a Jackie-like chignon, donning a one-shoulder beaded white gown with a dramatic white cape, and wore long white gloves.

There were other similarities.

Frank Sinatra organized the gala event at the Reagan inaugural in 1980, just as he had for the Kennedys. The only private inaugural party Mrs. Reagan attended was one thrown by journalist Nancy Dickerson at, of all places, Merrywood, the Virginia estate where Jackie had grown up (and which Dickerson and her husband later purchased).

Like Jackie, Mrs. Reagan set out to refurbish the White House. She also paid great attention to state dinners, turning them into lavish, star-studded events. She even hired Jackie's social secretary, Tish Baldrige, telling the *Washington Post* that she wanted Baldrige because "she knows how to do the same sort of thing I'm talking about."

But Mrs. Reagan's attempts to imitate Jackie backfired. The mood in America had changed dramatically by the time Ronald Reagan won the presidency. Mrs. Reagan even suffered by comparison to her role model. Whereas Jackie was praised for "restoring" a White House in need of a face-lift, Mrs. Reagan was pilloried for frivolously "redecorating." Nancy was portrayed in the press as greedy and shallow, more like what writer Tom Wolfe termed the social X-rays of New York—spoiled women who spend their days shopping, exercising, and visiting cosmetic surgeons—rather than the genteel young women of good taste and good breeding of Edith Wharton's high society to which Jackie was compared. Mockingly dubbed as "Queen Nancy" by the press, Mrs. Reagan was forced to rehabilitate her image by launching the "Just Say No to Drugs" campaign.

Although Hillary Clinton primarily tried to model herself after Eleanor Roosevelt, the most politically active First Lady in history, she asked Jackie for advice on how to raise her daughter, Chelsea, in the White House. Mrs. Clinton wanted desperately to provide the same kind of semblance of childhood normalcy for her daughter that Jackie provided for Caroline and John. At Jackie's funeral, Mrs. Clinton issued a statement praising her predecessor for her success in raising her children in the glare of public scrutiny. Mrs. Clinton traveled to Ravello, Italy, as had Jackie, where she visited Gore Vidal. He recalls that Hillary was fascinated by Jackie and wanted to talk endlessly about her. "I wonder," he wrote in his book *Palimpsest*, "if her interest in Jackie might not be genuine bewilderment at how a woman so selfish could be so beloved and Hillary, who wants actually to do something useful for others, is currently hated. Some obscure law of public relations is busily working overtime."

shelter outside Washington, and he wanted his wife to go ahead of him for her safety. But Jackie was unwilling to go, saying she wanted to remain with her husband instead.

That spring, Jackie became pregnant. She scaled back her official duties, though the pregnancy wasn't officially announced until April 18, 1963. The whole nation seemed swept up in excitement over the idea of having a pregnant First Lady: Not since Frances Cleveland had a president's wife been pregnant. In order to rest and relax, Jackie and the children spent the summer in a rented home on Squaw Island near Hyannis Port. But on August 7, just two days after the historic Nuclear Test-Ban Treaty was signed, tragedy struck. On the way back to the cottage from a horse-back riding lesson with Caroline, Jackie experienced severe cramping and immediately notified her doctor, who was vacationing nearby. He made arrangements for her to be transported by helicopter to the military hospital at Otis Air Force Base on Cape Cod.

Again Jackie underwent a Cesarean, giving birth to a boy, Patrick Bouvier. Five weeks premature, he weighed less than five pounds and suffered from a severe respiratory ailment often found in premature babies. Notified that Jackie was in labor, Jack flew to the Air Force base, arriving forty minutes after the birth of their new son.

The following day, the baby was moved to Children's Hospital in Boston, and then to the Harvard School for Public Health, where he was rushed into an oxygen chamber. Jack visited the child four times that day and slept that evening at the hospital, but Patrick's condition worsened overnight, and at 5:00 A.M. on August 9, 1963, he died. Jack returned to Otis Hospital to comfort Jackie, and there, brokenhearted by the loss of their child, the couple wept openly. Jackie wept to her husband, "There's only one thing I could not bear now—if ever I lost you."

The baby was buried at Holyrood Cemetery in Brookline, a few miles from the president's birthplace. Jackie sank into a deep depression. Jack devoted a great deal of time to trying to cheer her up, and bought the children, who were looking forward to a new baby brother, a cocker spaniel puppy. The tragedy seemed to draw the couple closer together.

The change in their marriage was evident on September 12, 1963, when the Kennedys celebrated their tenth anniversary with a party at Hammersmith Farm, where they had married. When Jack's helicopter landed on the lawn, Jackie ran up to greet him and, according to one of the guests, *Washington Post* editor Ben Bradlee, it was "the most affectionate embrace we had ever seen them give each other." For an anniversary gift, Jackie gave her husband three specially designed books documenting their years at the White House. She also gave him a gift with more emotional significance: a new St. Christopher's medal to replace the one he'd put in Patrick's coffin. Jack gave her a coiled serpent bracelet from Egypt.

Meanwhile, Jackie's sister, Lee, told her friend Aristotle Onassis, a Greek shipping magnate whom she had once dated, how depressed Jackie was about Patrick's death. Onassis suggested that a vacation might cheer her up and invited the two sisters for a cruise on his yacht *Christina*. Jack knew there would be some political fallout if his wife went; Onassis had been under investigation in the United States for alleged illegalities in his shipping business, and was openly having an extramarital affair with opera diva Maria Callas. The public was likely to look askance if the First Lady vacationed with him, but the president felt his wife needed the trip to recuperate, and he encouraged her to go.

Onassis, also aware of the political furor that might ensue, suggested that he would not go on the cruise. But Jackie insisted. "I could not accept his generous hospitality and then not let him come along," she said. "It would have been too cruel. I just couldn't have done that." Jack suggested that Under Secretary Franklin D. Roosevelt, a son of the former president, and his wife go along to make it politically more palatable.

Onassis's yacht was spectacular, complete with a crew of fifty, an orchestra for after-dinner dancing, two hairdressers, and a masseuse. Apparently nothing romantic occurred between Jackie and Ari on the trip. Jackie, who missed her husband terribly, kept saying that she wished Jack had been able to join them, and wrote him long letters. But there was no question that Onassis found his guest charming. The day of her departure he presented her with a diamond and ruby neck-lace as a parting gift.

Jackie was happy to return home. After a rocky start, Jack's presidency had become increasingly successful, at least in terms of public opinion. Already his advisers were beginning to plan for his reelection campaign. Jack was scheduled to take a political trip in November to Texas, where a rift between two factions of the local Democratic Party threatened his own chances of carrying the state in 1964. He had won it in 1960, but by only 46,233 votes, and he knew it would be close again, even with Lyndon Johnson on the ticket. Adlai Stevenson warned the president not to go: He had been there recently and found the crowds extremely antagonistic. But Kennedy's political advisers decided that a trip to Texas was essential, and Jack himself was determined to make it. Hoping to ease his reception, he asked his popu-lar wife to come along.

After thirteen trips abroad, Jackie may have felt that it was time for her to travel domestically. Or perhaps she agreed to accompany her husband because he had been so considerate after Patrick's death. Whatever the reason, on November 21, 1963, the couple boarded *Air Force One* for Dallas.

November 25, 1963

CHAPTER SIX

DALLAS

—◆—

The Kennedy White House expected an icy reception in Texas. But when they arrived in San Antonio, a cheering crowd of 125,000 greeted them with placards that read *"BIENVENIDO, MR. AND MRS. PRESIDENT"* and "JACKIE, COME WATER-SKIING IN TEXAS." In Houston there were even more well-wishers. The president's aide Dave Powers kidded him that his wife was a bigger draw than he was. "Mr. President, your crowd here was about the same as last year's," Powers said, adding wryly, "but a hundred thousand more people came out to cheer for Jackie." Jack knew that the surprisingly warm reception in Texas had much to do with his wife's popularity. "You see, you do make a difference," he told her proudly. It was hard to believe that this was the woman the Kennedys had feared would be a political liability. She had quickly become one of Jack's biggest assets, and along the way had earned his newfound respect.

Jack and Jackie spent the evening of November 21, 1963, at

a hotel in Fort Worth. When Jack emerged from the lobby the following morning, a group of people was already waiting outside, hoping to catch a glimpse of the glamorous First Couple. Jack obligingly went over to speak to them, but they demanded to see his wife. "Where's Jackie?" the crowd wanted to know. "Mrs. Kennedy is organizing herself," the president replied. "It takes a little longer, but, of course, she looks better than us when she does it."

Jackie had become an essential element in the Kennedy political machine. At a Chamber of Commerce meeting later that day, she arrived half an hour late, but the crowd still applauded approvingly when they saw her outfit: pink wool suit, pillbox hat, and white kid gloves. "Two years ago I introduced myself in Paris by saying I was the man who had accompanied Mrs. Kennedy to Paris," Kennedy told the animated crowd. "I am getting somewhat the same sensation as I travel around Texas. Why is it nobody wonders what Lyndon and I will be wearing?" Despite the worries and warnings, the trip was going beautifully.

Next stop: Dallas. Aboard *Air Force One*, the president's buoyant mood changed dramatically when he read an ad in the *Dallas News* that harshly criticized him for signing the Nuclear Test-Ban Treaty with the Soviet Union. Paid for by a right-wing group that called itself the "American Fact-finding Committee," the ad clearly disturbed the president. "We're heading into nut country today," he remarked to Jackie.

But the jubilant crowd that awaited their touchdown at Love Field in Dallas was hardly unwelcoming. Jackie was presented with a bouquet of red roses, and Jack worked the ropeline, shaking hands and exchanging pleasantries with some of the local residents who had turned out to cheer him on. The president was scheduled to deliver a luncheon address at the

Dallas Trade Mart, so they soon set off in a motorcade, heading toward the center of town. It was a swelteringly hot day, and Jackie, who was still wearing her wool suit, was uncomfortably hot. But the presidential limousine was a convertible, so there was a breeze as the motorcade made its way through the Dallas streets. Jack and Jackie sat in the backseat with the bouquet of roses between them, waving at the throngs of people lining the route. Nellie Connally sat with her husband, Governor John Connally, on a pull-out jump seat in front of the Kennedys. At one point she turned toward Jack and said, "You sure can't say that Dallas doesn't love you, Mr. President." "No," Jack replied, "you can't."

But at 12:30 P.M. CST, as the motorcade was passing slowly through Dealey Plaza in downtown Dallas, shots were fired and the president suddenly put both hands to his throat. Connally clutched his arm in pain and began screaming, "No, no, no!" The last shot hit Jack's skull with such explosive force that he slumped over into Jackie's lap, blood pouring from the bullet hole.

Jackie began screaming, "My God, what are they doing? My God, they've killed Jack, they've killed my husband!" Connally yelled, "God, they are going to kill us both." Terrified, Jackie scrambled back onto the trunk of the limousine, but Secret Service agent Clint Hill, who was running behing the car, managed to reach the trunk and push her back into the bloody rear passenger seat.

As the motorcade rushed to Parkland Memorial Hospital, Jackie held her dying husband, crying, "Jack, Jack, can you hear me? I love you, Jack." When they arrived at the hospital, she refused to let him be taken from her arms. "You know he's dead," she said to Clint Hill. "Leave me alone." She finally gave her husband up when Hill wrapped his suit jacket around

⬥ LYNDON JOHNSON ⬥

Jackie received a letter from Lyndon Johnson soon after the assassination. The new president said, "I only wish things could have been different—that I didn't have to be here. But the Almighty has willed differently, and now Lady Bird and I need your help. . . ."

Lyndon Johnson did everything in his power to remain on friendly terms with Jackie Kennedy. He had happily acquiesced to her every demand, changing the name of Cape Canaveral to Cape Kennedy. He regularly sent flowers to her, invited her to state dinners, and sent gifts to the children. He even offered her positions in the administration that might interest her, such as an ambassadorship or chief of protocol.

But Jackie could not be won over by her husband's successor. Although she was civil to Lady Bird, she had contempt for Lyndon. She refused his every invitation to the White House, did not attend his inaugural, and even declined his invitation to go to a ceremony where he was rededicating the Rose Garden in her honor. (She would not return to the White House until Nixon was in office.) If ever she saw Lyndon in public, she treated him like a pariah.

Franklin D. Roosevelt, Jr., was over at Jackie's one day when Lyndon called, attempting to woo her.

VICE PRESIDENT LYNDON JOHNSON IS SWORN IN AS PRESIDENT ABOARD *AIR FORCE ONE*, NOVEMBER 22, 1963.

Roosevelt told Heyman that Johnson called and said, "Sweetheart, listen, Lady Bird and I want to see you over here at our next White House dinner party. Jack was a great man, but you've got to start living again." Roosevelt said that Jackie was outraged. "How dare that oversize, cow-punching oaf call me 'sweetheart,'" she declared. "Who the hell does he think he is?" When Roosevelt told Johnson that Jackie was upset about how he had addressed her, Lyndon reportedly replied, "I'm tired as hell of this bullshit. Where I come from we call the ladies 'sweetheart,' and the ladies call their gentlemen 'honey.' I've bent over backward for that woman. I've done cartwheels and deep-knee squats and all I get is criticism."

Jackie had always looked down on the Johnsons. She could be considerate, at one point questioning why their names couldn't be announced along with the president's when "Hail to the Chief" was played. But she could also, on occasion, be rude. She thought they were hayseeds, nicknamed the vice president and his wife "Colonel Cornpone and his little pork chop," and often overlooked them when she was making out her guest lists for White House parties. When it was brought to her attention by chief of protocol Angier Biddle Duke that their feelings were hurt at having been excluded, she callously replied, "Good God, do I have to have them?"

She was no doubt influenced by her closest companion, Bobby, who had strong political differences with Johnson and who saw himself as a future political rival to the new president. Bobby believed that Johnson was an unworthy successor to his brother and felt that Johnson had behaved crudely after the assassination, too quickly taking over Jack's position (he gave the State of the Union message a day after the funeral) and taking credit for Jack's work. Bobby was furious at anyone who had any allegiance to Johnson.

In 1964, Jackie attended the Democratic National Convention as a show of support for Bobby, who was running in a tight race for the Senate. She wouldn't go near the convention center lest it be interpreted as a sign of support for Johnson. And the Johnson people didn't want her there. She was so popular with the American public that they feared she would go onto the floor, steal the convention away from Johnson, and turn it over to Bobby. Though Jackie's speech on the last night and a film about JFK, introduced by Bobby, provided the most emotional moments of the convention, Johnson did take the nomination and went on to defeat Barry Goldwater in the general election.

Jack's head. Jackie's own clothing, too, was drenched with blood, but she would not change. A doctor offered her a sedative to calm her down, but she refused to take it, asking instead to be allowed in the trauma room, where her husband was undergoing emergency surgery. The request was granted, and when she saw Jack on the operating table, she dropped to her knees and began to pray. When she rose, a doctor delivered the bad news: "Mrs. Kennedy, your husband has sustained a fatal wound."

"I know," she said softly.

The doctors placed a white sheet over Kennedy's body, leaving one of his feet sticking out. Jackie bent to kiss it. Then she pulled back the sheet and kissed his mouth, his eyes, and his hands. She clasped his hand and would not let go. Last rites were administered and at 2:31 P.M., the official announcement was made: The president had been assassinated. He was forty-six years old.

His body was placed in a bronze coffin. Jackie slipped her wedding band onto one of his fingers and sat beside his body in the back of the hearse as they made their way back to Love Field and *Air Force One*.

On the flight back to the capital, Lyndon Johnson was sworn in as the thirty-sixth president of the United States. He took the oath of office flanked by Jackie, who stood on his left, still in her bloodstained suit, and his wife, Lady Bird, who stood on his right. Jackie appeared to be in a state of shock, shedding no tears during the ceremony. But she was still thinking clearly. When asked again if she wanted to change out of her suit, she replied, "Let them see what they've done. I want them to see."

When the plane landed in Washington, Jack's brother Bobby was waiting with the news that "a Communist" had already been arrested in conjunction with the murder, a man named Oswald. To Jackie, this information made the crime seem more rather than less senseless. Jack had devoted himself to great causes, and she could hardly believe that he had been killed by a "silly little" Communist. There was no way to render the crime sensible or even understandable.

At Bethesda Naval Hospital, where the autopsy was conducted, Jackie was given a sedative, but it had no effect. When Secretary of Defense Robert McNamara arrived at the hospital late that evening, Jackie relayed the day's horrific events with meticulous precision. That evening, Janet and Hugh Auchincloss stayed at the White House, trying to comfort her. Jackie's sister, Lee, and her husband, Stas Radziwill, arrived shortly thereafter. Unbeknownst to the public, they brought a friend: Aristotle Onassis. All of them stayed at the White House.

John, Jr. and Caroline had to be told what had happened. Surprisingly, since Jackie was celebrated for the way she raised her children, she was not the one who told them their father had died. Perhaps the task was too difficult for her, so instead it was left to the nanny, Maude Shaw, who wept as she told Caroline. "I can't help crying, Caroline, because I have some very sad news to tell you," she said. "Your father has gone to look after Patrick. Patrick was so lonely in heaven. He didn't know anyone there. Now he has the best friend anyone could have." When John, Jr. was told that his father had gone to heaven, he asked, "Did he take his big plane with him?" Shaw replied, "Yes, John, he probably did." The little boy then said, "I wonder when he's coming back."

A few nights after the assassination, Jackie, unable to sleep, wrote a letter to her deceased husband, telling him how much she missed him. The next day, she asked Caroline and John, Jr. to do the same. John, Jr., too young to know how to write, made a drawing. His sister wrote a letter to their father, telling him how much she would miss him. In the meantime, the children had received a letter from President Johnson that explained how heroic their father had been.

In the interim, only two days after the arrest, Oswald had been shot and killed by Jack Ruby while being escorted by two policemen—and while national television cameras were rolling. Ruby claimed that he wanted to spare Mrs. Kennedy a return trip to Dallas for Oswald's trial. The country was devastated by JFK's death and the accompanying chaos, but Jackie herself remained remarkably composed in the immediate aftermath of the assassination. She devoted herself to orchestrating her husband's funeral, planning even the smallest details.

After the autopsy, Kennedy's coffin was placed in a catafalque in the East Room of the White House. Jackie's wedding band, which she had hastily slipped onto the president's finger, had been returned to her by a doctor who gently suggested that her husband would have wanted her to keep it. Although thankful, Jackie still wanted to leave something of sentimental value in her husband's coffin, so she replaced the ring with a bracelet that Jack had given her and some cuff links she had given to him. Bobby also left something for his brother: a tie pin commemorating the Navy boat Jack had skippered during the war, and an engraved silver rosary. As a memento for herself, Jackie cut a lock of Jack's hair.

Despite her grief, Jackie took control of the funeral arrangements, making sure that every detail was as she wanted it. While Jack's coffin lay in the East Room, Jackie requested the members of the honor guard posted there to stare directly at the coffin, although military protocol instructed that they should avert their eyes. Looking away, Jackie decided, was too cold.

Searching for a precedent, Jackie asked the chief of protocol

Jackie with her children and the Kennedy family at the funeral of her husband, November 25, 1963.

at the White House to send her material from the Library of Congress on President Lincoln's funeral. Perhaps Jackie believed that if she could incorporate elements from the funerals of great leaders, her husband's position would be elevated and his place in history secured. As when Lincoln was assassinated, she draped the White House in black and insisted that a riderless horse be incorporated into the ceremony.

She fought with the Kennedys about where Jack would be laid to rest. They wanted him to be buried in their family plot in Boston, but she insisted on Arlington National Cemetery, believing that he belonged to the country and not just his family. Jackie arranged to have the coffin of their stillborn daughter and son Patrick, who had lived for thirty-nine hours, disinterred and moved to Arlington, to be reburied with Jack. Inspired by the tomb of the Unknown Soldier under the Arc de Triomphe in Paris, she decided that an eternal flame should flicker over her husband's grave. During the ceremony, she would light the flame herself.

The day before the funeral, the president's coffin was moved from the White House to the Capitol rotunda, where it lay in state. The funeral itself, which took place on November 25, 1963, was broadcast live on national television. Jackie led the procession as Jack's brothers and his cabinet members, as well as world leaders, followed behind her. Clad in black mourning clothes, eyes swollen, the widowed First Lady brought John, Jr. and Caroline, both dressed in light blue coats and red lace-up shoes, to visit the flag-draped coffin. She explained to her six-year-old daughter, "We're going to say good-bye to Daddy and we're going to kiss him good-bye, and tell Daddy how much we love him and how much we'll always miss him." With great dignity and restraint, Jackie kissed the coffin in parting, but perhaps the most somber and unforgettable image from the day was provided by John, Jr., whose simple salute to the coffin as the procession passed engraved itself on the nation's collective memory.

Afterward, a reception for foreign dignitaries was held at the White House. Two hundred twenty representatives of one hundred and two nations, including eight chiefs of state and eleven heads of government, formed a long receiving line to express their sympathy to Mrs. Kennedy. One foreign official, however, was unimpressed by the pomp and circumstance of the funeral: Charles de Gaulle, who returned to France with very specific instructions about his own funeral, insisting that he be buried in a simple coffin with no public officials in attendance.

In the midst of all the grief, chaos, and drama, Jackie remained unruffled, so much so that she even threw a small birthday party for John, Jr., who was celebrating his third birthday that very day. Only family members and close friends were invited, and after the party, Bobby visited Jack's grave with Jackie, who left a bouquet of lilies of the valley.

One hundred million viewers tuned in to watch the funeral. The assassination and the funeral were unprecedented media events in American history, events the nation experienced together, all at once, by watching television. The death of a president, the grief of his widow, the poise of their children—the country shared in it all. The events transformed Jackie's image, making her, in some ways forever, beyond reproach.

❖ ❖ ❖

"You will be happy here."

After the funeral, Jackie knew she had to leave the White House. She was planning a temporary stay at a home owned by Mr. and Mrs. Averell Harriman, at 3038 Georgetown, a few blocks from the old Kennedy home. The Harrimans had graciously moved to a hotel until the former First Lady could find something permanent.

On November 26, the day after John Kennedy's funeral, Jackie invited Lady Bird Johnson to tea at the White House. "Don't be frightened of this house," Jackie told her successor. "Some of the happiest years of my marriage have been spent here. You will be happy here." Before she left the White House Jackie put up a plaque in the Lincoln bedroom, where she had slept, that read in part, "IN THIS ROOM LIVED JOHN FITZGERALD KENNEDY WITH HIS WIFE, JACQUELINE." It was placed beneath a plaque that said that Lincoln had slept in that room. Pat Nixon later removed the Kennedy plaque.

Jackie remained at the White House for eleven days before moving into the Harrimans' Georgetown home. Johnson provided Jackie and the family with Secret Service protection as well as the long-term loan of an eighteen-foot Coast Guard boat for Jackie's use, and Congress voted to provide her with office space for one year (the period was later extended) and a staff of her own choosing. A total of $50,000 was allocated for her office and staff expenses, but she wound up spending $120,000 more. Congress quickly approved the extra money.

Jack had left a total of $10 million in trust funds for both the children and Jackie, but she was only given yearly payments and did not have access to either of the funds directly. This is not to say that she was poor—far from it. Her annual income from the funds was $200,000, which was considerably more money than it is today. She also received an annual pension of $10,000, which was granted to presidents' widows for life or until they remarry, as well as free mailing privileges.

Even though she was only a member of the family by marriage, it was Jackie who would become the keeper of the Kennedy flame after her husband was assassinated. She dedicated a great deal of time to securing his place in history, and even long after she left the White House, Jackie still felt it necessary to preserve her late husband's public image. A week after the assassination, while spending Thanksgiving at Hyannis Port, she took it upon herself to call journalist Teddy White, who was then writing an article about the murder of the president for *Life*. She asked White if he would be interested in coming to the compound to have an interview with her. Of course, he was. The two spoke for four hours.

Jackie told White she had come to Hyannis Port for some solitude but also so she could tell Joe Kennedy, still ailing after his stroke, what had happened to his son. She and White discussed the exact sequence of events on the day of the assassination. According to White, the former First Lady remembered seeing "pink-rose ridges on the inside of the president's skull." Jackie said that "his head was so beautiful" and claimed "I tried to hold the top of his head down, maybe I could keep it in . . . but I knew he was dead." She said she regretted wiping off the blood and brain matter from her face before Lyndon Johnson was sworn in. "I wiped it off with a Kleenex . . . then one second later I thought, why did wash the blood off? I should have left it there, let them see what they've done. If I'd just had the blood and caked hair when they took the picture . . ."

She expressed no interest in finding out who the assassin was, according to White. The only thing that seemed to matter to her was the way Jack Kennedy's life and administration would be remembered. According to White, she had asked to speak to with him in order to "make certain that Jack was not forgotten in history." Jackie seemed to consider Jack's legacy best preserved in a realm beyond the historian's, as something more akin to an Arthurian legend than as simply an era in American politics. She confided to the journalist that at night she and Jack used to listen to the music from *Camelot* and Jack, according to his widow, personally identified with the theme song.

White later said that he realized at the time it was "a misreading of history." He explained, "At that moment, she could have sold me anything from an Edsel to the Brooklyn Bridge." It seemed to him that all Jackie desired was for him "to hang this *Life* epilogue on the Camelot conceit. It didn't seem like a

⬦ BOBBY ⬦

He is really very shy," Jackie once said of her brother-in-law Robert Kennedy. "But he has the kindest heart in the world." It is not surprising that Jackie felt warmly about Jack's younger brother Bobby. In the callous world of the Kennedys, Bobby stood out for his compassion. It was Bobby who came to Jackie's bedside in 1956 to deliver the news that her child had been born stillborn, to comfort her, and to arrange for the child's burial, while her husband was on a yacht in the Mediterranean. "You knew that if you were in trouble, he'd always be there," she said.

BOBBY ACCOMPANIES JACKIE AS THEY BRING THE BODY OF HER HUSBAND BACK TO WASHINGTON.

After the assassination, Jackie and Bobby grew very close. It wasn't long before the nature of the relationship became a matter of public speculation. As Laurence Leamer reports, "Staff members saw the candidate and Jackie walking hand-in-hand and whispered about the twosome, hoping that no photographer managed to take their picture. 'Jackie would call all the time and ask, 'Is Bobby there?' recalled one of his secretaries. 'The word we got was that she was shell shocked.' "

When Bobby considered leaving public service, it was Jackie who encouraged him to stay. Jackie wrote a letter to Bobby urging him not to abandon his political aspirations; he owed it to Jack to continue. She also said that she needed him, and that she was depending on him to be a surrogate father to her children.

She even allowed Bobby to be photographed with John and Caroline for his Senate race. Heymann also reports that in Jackie's later years in New York, people were struck that there was only one prominently displayed photo of a Kennedy in her apartment—and it was of Bobby.

hell of a lot. . . . So I said to myself, why not? If that's all she wants, let her have it."

In December, Jackie bought a house across the street from the Harrimans. Yet adjusting to civilian life in Washington was proving very difficult. She had become something of a tourist attraction; crowds gathered outside the house, and well-meaning strangers would call out to her or run over to the children to hug them. Furthermore, everything in Washington reminded her of her husband. Not surprisingly, she became very depressed. "Can anyone understand," she pleaded with friends, "how it is to have lived in the White House and then, suddenly, to be living alone?" Bobby seemed to be the only person able to console her, and the two became very close.

Ostensibly, she was now a private citizen. But she never really would be; the nation felt they owned a part of her, since they, too, shared in her grief and shock. Furthermore, Jackie still had some official business to take care of. In January 1964 she sweetly thanked the public on national television for the hundreds of thousands of condolence letters she had received. "The knowledge of the affection in which my husband was held by all of you has sustained me, and the warmth of these tributes is something that I shall never forget. Whenever I can bear to, I read them."

❧ ❧ ❧

"I hate this country."

Although she had purchased a home there, Jackie was coming to the conclusion that she could no longer live in Washington. The most logical choice for a new city was New York, where many famous people were able to live in relative anonymity. Jackie also had friends and family there; her sister and stepbrother Yusha both lived in New York, and Bobby moved there, too, to run for the Senate. So, in the summer of 1964, Jackie and the children moved into an elegant fourteen-room apartment at 1040 Fifth Avenue for which Jackie had paid $200,000. Once she had settled in, she began doing some work for the John F. Kennedy Memorial Library, which was being built in Boston, and helping Bobby with his political career.

In the summer of 1964 Jackie attended the Democratic National Convention in Atlantic City as a show of support for her brother-in-law. Bobby was considered by many to be the heir apparent to Jack. At the time he was campaigning for the Senate seat in New York, but it was already clear that he had plans in the near future to make a run for the presidency. Where once Jackie had felt neglected in the political arena, now she was the center of attention and she focused her energy on doing as much as possible for Bobby's senatorial campaign, even allowing him to be photographed with John, Jr.

On November 22, 1964, the first anniversary of JFK's death, *Look* magazine carried some comments from Jackie about her husband. Her grief had eased somewhat, and she was more wistful than angry when she spoke about her loss. "Now I think I should have known that he was magic all along," she said. "I did know it—but I should have guessed it could not last. I should have known that it was asking too much to dream that I might have grown old with him and seen our children grow up together. So now he is a legend when he would have preferred to be a man." Of course, much of that legend was of her creation.

In the meantime, Jackie had become embroiled in another battle to make Jack's White House years look good. Journalist

Jim Bishop, who had already written a book called *A Day in the Life of President Kennedy*, was planning to write another that would focus specifically on the assassination. Jackie didn't think Bishop was sufficiently ethical as a journalist and insisted that William Manchester, who was working on a similar book, titled *The Death of a President*, could be depended on to write the more accurate account. She cooperated with the journalist, giving him ten hours of interviews. But she would soon change her mind. She and Manchester would end up in a very public battle over the publication of his book, Jackie trying to get him to tone down passages in the book that she considered offensive.

Books were far from her only public relations problem. She became obsessed about anyone she knew speaking to the press about her. She adopted the Kennedy practice to make employees sign contracts saying they would not talk to the press.

In New York she began to mingle with a wealthier, more famous international set than she had in Washington. Among those she socialized with were author Philip Roth, literary bon vivant George Plimpton, and actor/director Mike Nichols. But even in New York, she could not escape attracting attention. Once, standing outside Bergdorf Goodman, Nichols said to Jackie, "Taking you anyplace is like going out with a national monument." "Yes," Jackie responded, "but isn't it fun?" Jackie had remained friendly with Aristotle Onassis throughout her years in New York. She saw him frequently; he would come to her apartment and bring expensive gifts for the children.

In March 1968 Robert Kennedy officially announced his candidacy for president. Jackie feared for his safety, particularly after Martin Luther King, Jr., was assassinated in April. At Bobby's request, Jackie attended Rev. King's funeral, which only seemed to intensify her worries about her brother-in-law.

*Jackie with Caroline and John, Jr. at Robert Kennedy's funeral,
June 1968.*

At a dinner party several weeks later, Jackie pulled Arthur
Schlesinger, Jr., aside, and said, "Do you know what I think
will happen to Bobby?" It was a rhetorical question. "The
same thing that happened to Jack. There is too much hatred in
the country, and more people hate Bobby than hated Jack."

Meanwhile, days after Bobby announced his candidacy,
Onassis was asked about Jacqueline Kennedy during an interview in Paris. He said of the former First Lady, "She is a
totally misunderstood woman. Perhaps she even misunder-
stands herself. She's being held up as a model of propriety,
constancy, and of so many of those boring American female

virtues. She's now utterly devoid of mystery. She needs a small scandal to bring her alive."

The paparazzi had been snapping photographs of Jackie with Onassis for some time. But because the wealthy but unattractive Onassis seemed such an unlikely romantic interest for the lovely former First Lady, few observers suspected that a serious attachment was developing between the pair.

Bobby knew otherwise, and guessed that they were planning to marry. He begged his sister-in-law not to wed the Greek shipping magnate until after the election; it could be a political liability for him. Jackie, by now long accustomed to those kinds of political calculations, agreed to put off any long-term romantic plans until November 12, when the votes would already have been cast. She and Onassis continued to see each other but tried to keep their liaisons more discreet.

Onassis, perhaps to ingratiate himself with the Kennedy family, made a healthy contribution to Bobby's campaign. In June Bobby's campaign gathered steam with a major win in the California primary. After delivering his victory speech to supporters at a hotel in Los Angeles, Bobby was shot as he made his way through the hotel galley. The assassin was a young Palestinian named Sirhan Sirhan, who claimed he was retaliating for the Arabs' defeat in the Six-Day War. When she heard the news, Jackie, who was in New York at the time, immediately flew to California to be at Bobby's bedside. But she didn't get there in time. Bobby Kennedy died a day after being shot, on June 6.

The loss of Bobby was more than Jackie could take. "I hate this country," she said the day after Bobby's funeral. "I despise America and I don't want my children to live here anymore. If they're killing Kennedys, my kids are number one targets. . . . I want to get out of this country."

October 20, 1968

CHAPTER SEVEN

JACKIE O.

◆

Famous, beautiful, clever, sophisticated—it might seem that Jackie might have no shortage of suitors. But, in fact, these very qualities made it difficult for her to find the right man to marry. She would overshadow almost any man she met, and most would be daunted by her status. She was the widow of one of the most admired presidents in recent history. She was American royalty—not just a Kennedy, but also the self-styled queen of Camelot.

Aristotle Onassis was an attractive match for Jackie in many ways, not least because the Greek shipping magnate happened to be one of the wealthiest men in the world. Over the years Jackie had developed expensive tastes. For her, the money her husband had left her wasn't enough to enable her to live in the style to which she had become accustomed. Of course, she could always go, and often did, to the Kennedys for extra money. But any money she received from the Kennedys came with strings attached: She was expected to attend official events, and she felt beholden to the family that had withheld its approval of her. She was desperate to break loose from the web of responsibilities that being a Kennedy, and living off Kennedy money, entailed. She was also worried about the emotional problems that might develop if the children grew up without a father figure. John, Jr. was already having some trouble. His teachers had recommended he repeat first grade, but Jackie insisted that he be allowed to move on.

As a foreigner, Onassis wasn't as awed by the Kennedy mystique. Twenty-three years older than Jackie, he was also a strong, intelligent, powerful, and charismatic man. He had his own persona, and it had nothing to do with her. Jackie, ever the Europhile, found his cosmopolitan élan seductive.

Yet no matter how much sense the match made to Jackie, there was no question the public would disapprove if America's tragic sweetheart married a foreigner—and an unattractive one at that. Short and homely, Onassis was quite a contrast to the handsome, All-American Jack Kennedy. Onassis was also divorced and a member of the Greek Orthodox Church. The Vatican would never approve of the marriage and Jackie risked excommunication, which she cared about more for the children's sake than her own. Furthermore, Onassis had legal problems in the United States: In 1954 he had been indicted on criminal charges involving his shipping business and forced to pay a $7 million fine to avoid a trial. Finally, he had a reputation for womanizing: His extramarital affair with Maria Callas had been splashed all over the pages of American tabloids. Of course, Jack Kennedy also had had many such liaisons, but the public wasn't aware of them at the time.

Jackie's own relatives also found the match unsavory. Her mother, for instance, was vehemently opposed. Janet Auchincloss believed Onassis wasn't genteel enough for Jackie, and she disliked the fact that he had formerly dated Jackie's sister, Lee. Onassis reminded Janet of her own former husband, Black Jack, and she harbored suspicions that her thirty-nine-year-old daughter was marrying a sixty-two-year-old man in an attempt to replace her father. For their part, the Kennedys didn't want anything to tar their reputation. They were particularly worried that if Jackie married outside the Catholic faith, it would be politically harmful to them. Surprisingly, however, Rose Kennedy was very much in favor of the marriage. She liked Onassis personally, and perhaps she also looked forward to her daughter-in-law having another source of money besides the Kennedy fortune. But before they would give their approval to the wedding, the Kennedys made Jackie promise that John, Jr. and Caroline would be raised and schooled in the United States.

That fall, Jackie had an important meeting with Cardinal Cushing, who said that although the Vatican would never approve, he felt she should remarry if it meant moving on with her life, and that he would publicly defend her remarriage. Getting the approval of Cushing, who had married Jack and Jackie, was crucial to her own peace of mind. She wanted his blessing and she wanted to know that her children would still have a place in the American Catholic Church. Lee, who had formerly dated Onassis herself, was another who supported her sister's decision to remarry. "Americans can't understand a man like Onassis," she said. "If my sister's new husband had been blond, young, rich, and Anglo-Saxon, most Americans would have been much happier, I suppose."

Whatever opposition she faced, however, it was nothing compared to the disapproval Onassis was facing from his teenage children—Alexander and Christina. They begged their father not to marry Jackie. They were still very loyal to their mother, Tina, and despised Maria Callas for breaking up their parents' marriage; they felt much the same about Jackie. Alexander, in particular, believed the former First Lady's interest in his father was purely mercenary, and dubbed her "the widow" and "the American geisha." Ari thought this behavior was typical for children whose parents had divorced, and paid scant attention to their pleas, complaints, and insults.

Maria Callas, too, was miserable about the match. She and Ari had had a very passionate love affair, and she believed Jackie's relationship with him was devoid of emotion. Though privately crushed, she tried to refrain from public criticism. On occasion, however, she slipped, as when she snidely commented that "Jackie did well to give a grandfather to her children."

Despite all these arrayed forces of disapproval, Ari and Jackie went ahead with their plans to marry. Once the Kennedys saw that they couldn't stop Jackie, they were determined to ensure that she got the best financial deal possible. Teddy Kennedy was designated to go on a trip with Ari aboard his yacht to negotiate the prenuptial contract. Once Jackie remarried she would lose her income from the Kennedy trust as well as her $10,000 annual widow's pension and Secret Service protection. Onassis promised the Kennedys that she would not suffer financially if she married him and that he would provide the necessary security for Jackie and the children.

As part of the prenuptial contract, Onassis, whose fortune was estimated at $500 million, asked her to waive her inheritance rights under Greek law, which stipulated that a husband must leave his wife at least 12.5 percent of his estate. In return, he gave Jackie $3 million right away to bank or to convert to nontaxable bonds. He also placed $1 million each in trust funds for the children and promised to give them the interest until they were twenty-one. In the event of his death or a divorce, Jackie was guaranteed an additional $200,000 a year. But those were just the formal monetary benefits. There were other rewards as well. Onassis, an exceedingly generous man, presented his fiancée with a heart-shaped ruby and diamond engagement ring worth $1.25 million.

Once the prenuptial agreement was signed, the wedding plans were officially announced to the public. On October 17, 1968, Nancy Tuckerman, who was still serving as Jackie's press secretary, read a statement to the media: "Mrs. Hugh D. Auchincloss has asked me to tell you that her daughter, Mrs. John F. Kennedy, is planning to marry Aristotle Onassis sometime next week."

When rumors of their financial arrangements began to surface in the news, the public, not surprisingly, concluded that Jackie was marrying not for love but for money. Even Onassis joked about the high price he'd paid for his bride. "I did not expect a dowry," he told friends after his meeting with Teddy, "and I did not get one." Quite the opposite, in fact.

The press launched into a convulsion. Reporters clamored for access to the ceremony, but Jackie refused. "We wish our wedding to be a private moment in the little chapel among the cypresses of Skorpios, with only members of the family and their children," she said in a statement released to the press. But, of course, the press was not going to take no for an answer. In the end, Ari and Jackie allowed four reporters to write accounts of the wedding that could be distributed to the rest of the press.

Jackie and Ari were married by a Greek Orthodox priest on the afternoon of October 20, 1968. Hugh Auchincloss again gave Jackie away, but otherwise her second wedding was quite unlike the first: very small and simple. John, Jr. and Caroline were there, as were Janet and Hugh Auchincloss, Lee and Stas Radziwill and their children, and a smattering of Kennedy relatives. Onassis had spontaneously flown the guests to the Greek island of Skorpios on a private chartered plane belonging to the airline his family owned, Olympic Airways. Jackie wore a long-sleeved lace Valentino dress that ended mid-thigh and low heels so she wouldn't tower over her fiancé, and a ribbon in her hair. John, Jr. and Caroline held candles, but it was not a particularly romantic event—the couple did not even kiss during the ceremony.

The reception afterward was held aboard Ari's yacht, the *Christina*, on which Jackie had vacationed in 1963 after her son Patrick's death. For this happy occasion she wore a floor-length white skirt and black blouse, but most striking was her jewelry: more than a million dollars' worth, all gifts from the bridegroom. The *Christina* was lavish and enormous: Larger than a football field, it contained a small movie theater and a swimming pool. But it was the decor that attracted the most media attention. The pink marble bathrooms, the bar stools made of whale scrotums, the naked little girls on the dining room wallpaper all seemed vulgar and gaudy, especially when compared to the sleek, classic style epitomized by Jackie herself.

The day after the wedding, newspapers around the world were damning. "HOW COULD YOU?" read one headline. Another said, "JACKIE WEDS BLANK CHECK," Even the staid *New York Times* wrote: "The reaction here is anger, shock, and dismay." If anything, this was an understatement. All across Ireland, Jackie's picture was removed from the walls of pubs. Hate mail arrived daily at her Fifth Avenue apartment, and she was regularly ridiculed and chastised by the media. Journalists were unanimous: She had married for money. They gave the fallen former First Lady a nickname befitting her new status: "Jackie O."

Almost overnight, she went from being a symbol of good taste to being an emblem of greed, but it didn't seem to faze Jackie. She had anticipated the negative reaction she would receive from the normally adoring public, but felt it was time to stop worrying about what others thought and do what felt right to her. After Jack Kennedy's death, she had confided to Ben Bradlee and his wife, Tony, that she would never marry again. "I consider that my life is over," she wrote in a letter to the couple, "and will spend the rest of it waiting for it really to be over." But after five years of widowhood, her reasoning had changed. She was only thirty-nine, surely young enough to deserve a second chance at love. For her, the Kennedy mystique had become something of a trap. When an acquaintance warned that the marriage would knock her off the pedestal the public had created for her, Jackie replied, "That's better than freezing there."

❧ ❧ ❧

"Jackie is like a little bird . . ."

The first year of the marriage was quite happy. Jackie had always struggled with the feeling that she wasn't as wealthy as those around her, and for the first time in her life, that insecurity evaporated. Onassis had seventy-two servants in his home in Skorpios. He had estates and villas all over the world. The day after the wedding, Jackie began taking advantage of her new wealth. After Ari went on a business trip to Athens and all the guests departed, she invited New York decorator Billy Baldwin to fly to the island to give her some advice on how to

Jackie and Ari.

redecorate her new residence. The advice alone ended up
costing Onassis $25,000, but he didn't seem to mind. At first
he put up with, and sometimes even encouraged, her shopping
sprees. He felt Jackie had suffered so much in her life that she
deserved to be taken care of and indulged. He showered her
with expensive gifts and gave her carte blanche with his
credit cards.

Onassis seemed pleased with his new marriage. He rarely
saw his former flame Maria Callas, even though he and Jackie
spent little time together. She was constantly shuttling back
and forth between Europe and the United States, where her
children were in school, but Ari didn't seem to mind that their
lives were so separate. "Jackie is like a little bird that needs

its freedom as well as its security," he told one interviewer. "And she gets both from me. . . . I never question her and she never questions me."

Onassis also proved to be a very good stepfather to Caroline and John. Not only was he very generous, he also seemed to genuinely care for them. He looked after them when they were sick, attended their school plays, and took them to baseball games. The children seemed to like him, too.

Jackie, however, did nothing to endear herself to Onassis's children. She was especially critical of Christina, who suffered from low self-esteem and took tranquilizers for depression and amphetamines to lose weight. Jackie regularly found fault with Christina's appearance, telling her she was too heavy and should have electrolysis to remove excess body hair. Perhaps she believed this was helpful advice, but whatever her intentions, Jackie's comments only made her stepdaughter dislike and distrust her even more.

Jackie's newfound wealth enabled her to gain some distance from the Kennedy clan, but because of the children, there was still a great deal of contact. The first year of her marriage was a bad one for the Kennedys. That was the year of Teddy's infamous and tragic night at Chappaquiddick with Mary Jo Kopechne, a former aide to his brother Bobby. Late at night, on July 18, 1969, Teddy was driving with Kopechne on the island off Martha's Vineyard when his car careened off a little bridge into the water below. Teddy escaped serious injury, but Kopechne drowned. It would have been a public relations nightmare anyway because he was a married man out with a young, attractive, single woman, but Teddy compounded the difficulties by not immediately reporting the accident to the police. Instead he phoned family members asking how he should deal with the fallout—and one of the first calls he made was to Jackie. He never reached her. Joe Kennedy, the family patriarch and the Kennedy with whom Jackie was closest, died not long after he heard about the incident on July 18. He was eighty-one.

Teddy's scandalous behavior only seemed to heighten interest by the press and the public in all things Kennedy. Jackie was constantly hounded by the paparazzi. Unquestionably, the photographer she most despised was Ron Galella, who covered her for years and was responsible for some of the most beautiful photographs ever taken of Jackie. Galella was always lurking around trying to snap photographs of her and the children. Once, in 1969, when Jackie went bicycling with John, Jr. in Central Park, Galella suddenly materialized and took their picture, startling John, Jr. so much that he momentarily lost control of his bicycle and almost got into an accident. Another time, Galella trailed Caroline at a school carnival.

In the fall of 1969 Jackie had Galella arrested and sued him, claiming that he was causing her family "grievous mental anguish." She sought a permanent injunction to keep him away from her. He filed a counterclaim, seeking $1.3 million in punitive damages for false arrest, malicious persecution, and interference with his livelihood as a photographer. His counterclaim was dismissed and he was instructed to remain 150 feet away from Jackie, 225 feet away from her children, and 300 feet away from her Fifth Avenue apartment. The ruling handicapped Galella but it didn't stop him: He simply resorted to using a long lens and continued to photograph the family.

Onassis thought this legal battle with Galella was ridiculous. Like JFK, he believed media attention was a natural by product of fame, and refused to pay the legals bills for the trial, which amounted to $500,000. Meanwhile, Jackie's legal skirmish with Galella only spurred on other reporters and photographers.

Once, while she and Onassis sunbathed nude on Skorpios, a group of European paparazzi, who were far more aggressive than American photographers, used telephoto lenses and underwater cameras to take pictures of the couple. The photos were sold for princely sums to men's magazines and eventually appeared in numerous tabloids around the world. Jackie was infuriated—and mortified.

❧ ❧ ❧

"I always lived in a dream world."

By 1970, after just two years, the marriage was beginning to unravel. Ari was having family troubles, particularly with his children. Although arranged marriages were common in wealthy Greek families, Christina didn't want to marry the man her father chose for her—Peter Goulandris, the twenty-three-year-old scion of another wealthy shipping family and whom she had known since childhood. Instead, Christina decided to marry a forty-eight-year-old Los Angeles realtor, Joe Bolker, whom she had met at a swimming pool in Monte Carlo. Onassis was adamantly opposed to the marriage; Bolker was twice divorced, had four children, and was not particularly well off. Ari threatened to disinherit his daughter if she continued to see him. In defiance, Christina eloped and moved to L.A. with Bolker. (Jackie sent them a congratulatory note.) After a short period of time, the marriage ended and Christina moved back to Greece. Ari relented and reinstated her in his will.

In the meantime, Alexander had fallen in love with Fiona Campbell Thyssen, a Scottish-born model who was divorced

❖ LEE ❖

Like many sisters, there was a mixture of love and rivalry in the relationship between Jackie and Lee. Although both attractive, as children they had very different personalities. Lee was warm and cuddly, whereas Jackie was cold and independent. Lee was her mother's favorite and Jackie was her father's, although the two little girls competed fiercely for Black Jack's attention.

Lee turned into a beautiful teenager. She was very stylish, had a curvaceous figure, and got lots of attention from men, constantly upstaging her older sister. Like Jackie, she was named Debutante of the Year. Lee made it to the altar before Jackie. In April 1953 she married Michael Canfield, the adopted son of publisher Cass Canfield. "Lee was always the pretty one," Jackie said years later. "I guess I was supposed to be the smart one." Later in life, Lee would continue to get much attention from men, including Jack Kennedy. If Jackie was unable to travel on state trips abroad, Jack would often ask Lee to accompany him in her stead. It was Lee who stood beside Kennedy when he made his famous *Ich bin ein Berliner* speech in Germany.

But it was Lee who was forced to live in Jackie's shadow as an adult. In 1959, Lee divorced Canfield, and with the help of her presidential brother-in-law she had the marriage annulled. She went on to marry Prince Stanislas Radziwill. (She had two children with him: Anthony and Christina.) Lee now had the title of princess but it was Jackie who truly occupied that position.

As her sister captivated the world, Lee was relegated to being known as "Jackie's sister." What made things worse was that as an adult, Lee was floundering. She had a brief but unsuccessful stint as an actress, starring as Tracy Lord in a stage production of *The Philadelphia Story* and appearing in a television remake of the 1944 film *Laura*. "Pathetic, lamentable, and sad" was how one reviewer described her performance in *The Philadelphia Story*.

As children they had grown closer because of their parents' divorce, had banded together as outsiders in the Auchincloss household. They traveled together as teenagers, and Lee was Jackie's closest friend while she was in the White House. During her Onassis years, Lee was very supportive of her sister and saw her frequently. "Lee was the only woman Jackie ever felt truly comfortable with," said a friend.

and sixteen years his senior. Ari wanted his wife's support to deal with these problems, but she was rarely there. Jackie spent far more time in the United States than with him, and her husband believed he would never be a top priority in her life. She was still bound too closely to the Kennedys—and to her former role as First Lady.

This was true, although Jackie often refused to attend official events. She did, however, return to the White House for the first time on February 3, 1971, during Richard Nixon's first term for a private viewing of Aaron Shikler's White House portraits of Jack and Jackie. The former First Lady did not attend the official unveiling of the portraits. Instead, she and her children had a private dinner with the Nixons. At one point during their conversation Jackie told Nixon, "I always lived in a dream world." And in this world, apparently, the rough-edged man she had married had no place.

Undoubtedly, Jackie and Ari were very different. Despite his wealth, he was simple and somewhat unsophisticated, and Jackie complained constantly about his bad taste in clothes and crass manners. Perhaps because she was bored or unhappy, her spending increased to the point where it was completely out of control. Much like her father, Black Jack, she spent money compulsively, racking up bills of $20,000 to $30,000—each month.

By the end of 1972 it was clear the marriage would not last. The final straw came on January 22, 1973, when Onassis's son, Alexander, who had just turned twenty-four, was killed in a private plane crash. Alexander was heir and successor to the Onassis fortune, and his father was shattered by the loss. Jackie, however, remained cold and composed. It is unclear whether her impassive reaction was a result of her poor relationship with Alexander, or whether it was simply the way she had learned to deal with death. Although there was no evidence to support this theory, Onassis became convinced that foul play was involved in his son's death. Jackie tried to persuade him that this notion was irrational and counterproductive: A conspiracy theory would not bring back his son.

After his son's death, Onassis's feelings toward Jackie changed abruptly. Since she seemed inept at consoling him, Onassis turned to Maria Callas for solace and also began to spend time again with his ex-wife, Tina, who shared his grief most fully. Onassis never completely recovered from Alexander's death. He sold Olympic Airways, since flying was the activity that had robbed him of his son. Perhaps because of the strain that he was under, Onassis became ill, developing a nerve and muscle disorder called myasthenia gravis, and Jackie became increasingly unhappy in the marriage. In January 1974 Ari rewrote his will, now convinced that Alexander had been right in thinking that Jackie had married him for his money. In the new will Ari left her the minimum amount outlined in their prenuptial contract and named Christina the prime beneficiary. To prepare his daughter to manage the vast fortunes she would one day inherit, he began training her to take over his financial affairs.

On September 10, 1974, Onassis's ex-wife, Tina, died of lung disease. Christina, miserably unhappy at the loss of both her brother and her mother, attempted suicide. Apparently she blamed Jackie for the deaths. Biographer Stephen Birmingham wrote, "To Christina it seemed as though Jackie killed every life she touched. She was the Angel of Death. This terrible conviction was all the more powerful because, by then, Christina could see that her father was also dying." She began to call Jackie "the Black Widow."

Jackie might not have been living with her husband, but she

was still spending his money quite freely. On one excursion she allegedly bought two hundred pairs of shoes and presented a bill to Onassis for $60,000. Ari reached an inescapable conclusion: "She wants my money but not me."

Onassis wanted to file for divorce but was afraid that public sympathy would be so much on the side of the former First Lady that he would lose a large part of his fortune in the process. He felt the public didn't understand how he was being victimized and exploited, so he solicited American investigative reporter Jack Anderson to write a story about Jackie's outrageous spending. He supplied the journalist with the necessary bills and documentation to verify the allegation. When the story checked out, Anderson called Nancy Tuckerman for a response. "We will not dignify those charges with a comment," said Tuckerman.

Onassis set divorce proceedings in motion. In the fall of 1974 Jackie got a call: Her husband was dying. He was admitted to the American hospital at Neuilly-sur-Seine in Paris, but Jackie was rarely at his bedside. In fact, the week he died, attempts were made to notify her that the end was near, but no one could locate her. Only Christina and Ari's sisters were at the hospital. Maria Callas was permitted a last visit with her lover, but he had degenerated so quickly that he could barely recognize her. When Onassis died on March 15, 1975, Jackie was in New York.

On March 18 Jackie, Teddy Kennedy, and Christina flew to Greece for the funeral. It was a simple service. In accordance with Ari's wishes, no eulogy was delivered. Jackie knelt and kissed the coffin but showed no signs of outward distress. Christina, however, was inconsolable and began weeping uncontrollably when her father's coffin was lowered into the grave beside her brother's.

Jackie with stepdaughter Christina Onassis.

In Athens following the funeral, Jackie released a statement to the press: "Aristotle Onassis rescued me at a time when my life was engulfed in shadows. He brought me into a world where one could find both happiness and love. Nothing has changed in [my relationship] with Aristotle's sisters and his daughter. The same love binds us as when he lived." Christina didn't feel quite as charitable. She aledgedly told a friend, "What amazes me is that she survives while everybody around her drops. She's dangerous, she's deadly. She has decimated at least two families—the Kennedys and mine. If I never see her again it will be too soon."

When asked by a reporter whether she thought there would be a battle over the $1 billion estate, Jackie replied, "Throughout the world, people love fairy tales and especially those related to the lives of the rich. You must learn to understand this and accept it."

The *New York Times* reported that before he died, Ari had planned to divorce Jackie. Jackie asked Christina to refute the story. She did, fearing pressure from the Kennedy clan. She released her own statement to the press: "Miss Christina Onassis is very much distressed at the distorted stories and speculations which appeared in the international press about her father and Mrs. Jacqueline Onassis. These stories are totally untrue and she repudiates them. In fact, the marriage of the late Mr. Onassis and Mrs. Jacqueline Kennedy was a happy marriage and all rumors of intended divorce arc untruc. Her relationship with Mrs. Onassis was always and still is based on mutual friendship and respect, and there are no financial or other disputes separating them."

Jackie and Christina subsequently became involved in an eighteen-month battle over Ari's estate. Jackie's lawyers tried to prove that Ari's most recent will was invalid. Christina finally settled out of court, offering Jackie $26 million to drop the case. In the six years that Jackie was married to Onassis, she received an estimated $42 million.

September 1975

CHAPTER EIGHT

THE FINAL YEARS

After Onassis's death, Jackie moved back to New York permanently. She had spent most of her adult life in the public eye defined by the men she had married. It was unclear to many observers what she would do next; whether she would return to the Kennedy family and the American political scene or remain part of the international jet set. As it turned out, she did neither. Instead of falling back on her past, she re-created herself, as so many other women her age did in the 1970s. She became a working mother.

Perhaps encouraged by President Ford's executive order declaring 1975 International Women's Year, Jackie decided to get a part-time job. After all, John, Jr. and Caroline were teenagers, and they no longer needed as much attention as they had when they were younger. Offers flooded in for the former First Lady. NBC wanted her to host a TV special on artifacts from Venice and Angkor Wat. The publisher of the *New*

York Post, Dorothy Schiff, urged Jackie to run for the New York Senate seat held by Republican James Buckley. Jackie's friend and former social secretary, Tish Baldrige, suggested that Jackie's skills—she wrote well and had a flair for design—would be well suited to the publishing industry. The idea of working in the publishing world appealed to Jackie, so Baldrige set up appointments for her with people in the industry. One of the meetings was with Thomas H. Guinzburg, the president of Viking Press, whose acquaintance Jackie had first made years before through Lee.

"I recognized what a boon she could be to a publishing firm," Guinzburg later said. "She had access to a wide range of interesting and important figures. She knew literally everyone, and in publishing it's not so much what but whom you know." Guinzburg snapped her up immediately, then arranged a press conference to announce that Jacqueline Onassis would join Viking in early September 1975, when she would begin working four days a week for an annual salary of $10,000, standard pay for an entry-level position. The press reported that although Jackie had an assistant, her office was small and unfurnished. Her colleagues were generally supportive, if a bit awed. "She didn't know a lot about how to put a book together at first," said one Viking coworker, "but she was willing to roll up her sleeves and learn."

Jackie primarily worked on expensive coffee table books. But her time at Viking was not without controversy. One of her first undertakings was a book called *Remember the Ladies: Women of America, 1815*. Three years after its release, Gloria Steinem wrote an article in *Ms.* glorifying Jackie as a modern career woman. She reported that Jackie had been responsible not only for the book's acquisition but also for its content. The book's author, historian and university professor Linda Grant

De Pauw, was incensed by the article and wrote a letter to the editor saying that Jackie had, in fact, played a small, if nonexistent, role in the book's production. But by all accounts, though, Jackie did play a large role in producing some of the books she worked on at Viking.

In 1977 Jackie left Viking after a controversy erupted over a novel by Jeffrey Archer titled *Shall We Tell the President?* In the book, Teddy Kennedy is president and is the target of an assassination attempt. A *New York Times* review criticized Jackie for allowing the novel to be published. "Anybody associated with its publication should be ashamed of herself," read the last line of the review. Although Jackie was aware that the book was being published, she had deliberately not read it. In fact, Guinzburg had advised against it. Later Guinzburg released a statement that said that Jackie had not made any objections to the book's acquisition from its British publisher. Outraged at the suggestion that she was in some way responsible for the book being published, Jackie quit.

Rival publishing house Doubleday, where her friend Nancy Tuckerman worked, immediately offered her a job as an associate editor. Jackie accepted, and remained at Doubleday for the rest of her career. In 1982 she was promoted to full editor. One of her strengths was luring celebrities to Doubleday, and her biggest coup came in 1984, when she persuaded Michael Jackson to write his memoirs, *Moonwalk*. He agreed to the project on one condition: Jackie, who he felt would be sensitive to his privacy, had to be the editor. Jackie agreed.

During this period of her life, Jackie almost never dabbled in politics, although she did become something of a social activist. Gloria Steinem tried to convince her to become more involved with the women's movement. Although Jackie generously donated money to the *Ms.* Foundation and supported the

Equal Rights Amendment, she would not join public ERA demonstrations. Nevertheless, in 1979, in a special issue, "Why Women Work," she did write an article for *Ms.* testifying to her support for the feminist movement. "What has been sad for many women of my generation," she wrote, "is that they weren't supposed to work if they had families. There they were, with the highest education, and what were they to do when the children were grown—watch the raindrops coming down the windowpane?" Jackie also continued to show an interest in historic preservation, serving as an influential member of the board of the Municipal Art Society in New York. At the urging of former New York Giant football star Rosie Grier, Jackie also became involved in a program called Giant Step, a charity devoted to helping inner city youth.

When she first returned to New York, Jackie had continued to maintain at least some contact with the Kennedys. But as time went on, Jackie grew estranged from the Kennedy clan, never going to Hyannis Port for Christmas or Thanksgiving and rarely attending the weddings of her many nieces and nephews. In 1990 she chose not to join the 350 guests who celebrated Rose's one-hundredth birthday at Hyannis Port, electing instead to remain just across the water on Martha's Vineyard to help her friend Carly Simon promote a new book. Perhaps Jackie kept her distance in part because she didn't want her own children to fall under the influence of what she apparently saw as their spoiled and unruly Kennedy cousins. She had little interest in helping the Kennedys with their political races

Despite her disaffection from the rest of the Kennedys, she stayed close to Teddy and made a point of taking part in commemorative events for both Jack and Bobby. Every year she would attend the Robert F. Kennedy pro-celebrity tennis tournament held in Forest Hills, New York. In 1979 she was present at the opening ceremony of the John F. Kennedy Memorial Library in Boston with her children. And she would make regular pilgrimages to Arlington National Cemetery to visit the graves of her husband and brother-in-law.

She was also friendly with Teddy's wife, Joan, empathizing with her struggle to try to fit into the Kennedy family. Joan often sought Jackie's advice. When Joan discovered that Teddy had been having affairs, she sought her sister-in-law's counsel. Jackie told her not to let it bother her. "Kennedy men are like that," she told Joan. "They'll go after anything in skirts. It doesn't mean a thing." But Joan didn't agree. She and Teddy divorced. Later on in life, Joan, after having a boyfriend die in an accident, complained to Jackie that life had been unfair to her. "Joan," Jackie said, "do you really expect life to be fair after everything we've gone through?"

Jackie's own family had been facing adversity on several fronts since her stepfather Hugh Auchincloss's death in 1976. Much of his money had been lost in a series of bad real-estate deals, and Jackie's mother, Janet, was forced to sell both Hammersmith Farm and Merrywood and move to the former servants' quarters, a twelve-room house on the Merrywood estate. Jackie established a $1 million trust fund so that her mother, who eventually married for a third time, could live out her life comfortably. Hammersmith Farm, their summer home in Newport, was turned into a tourist attraction run by a firm called Camelot Gardens. In 1984, at the age of thirty-nine, Jackie's half sister, Janet, died of bone marrow cancer, and shortly thereafter, Jackie's mother developed Alzheimer's disease. Despite their tense relationship for most of their lives, Jackie was very supportive of her mother during this time, often visiting her and regularly sending her

✦ GREY GARDENS ✦

GREY GARDENS.

While Jackie lived in luxury, some members of her family were not faring so well. Her aunt, Edith Bouvier Beale (Black Jack's sister), had always been eccentric. But over the years, she had slowly gone mad. Abandoned by her husband, she and her equally eccentric daughter, Edie, lived together at Grey Gardens, their family estate in East Hampton. Edie, a beautiful ex-debutante twelve years Jackie's senior, had wanted to be a dancer. Edith spent most of her day in bed singing operettas, surrounded by her many cats.

Edith and little Edie were unable to care for themselves or for the once-stately twenty-eight-room Grey Gardens, which by the end of the 1970s had become dilapidated. There

were cats everywhere and `the floor was littered with excrement. The stench was overpowering. Cobwebs blocked the windows and high grass had replaced the manicured lawns. There was no heat or running water in the house. Edith had had a dispute with the Sanitation Department, so the garbage was occassionally not picked up for months.

In 1971, at the urging of the neighbors, the Suffolk County Health Department came in to investigate. Upon seeing the inside of the home, investigators declared it a health hazard. They even found a dead cat in Edith's bedroom. A call was placed to Bouvier Beale, Edith's son, a wealthy New York lawyer, to tell him that unless Grey Gardens was fixed up, the two women would be evicted. But Bouvier Beale refused to finance the repairs, believing that it was in the best interest of his mother and sister to be removed from the house and given proper care. Within days, the national press discovered that Edith Beale was related to Jackie. "JACKIE'S AUNT TOLD: CLEAN UP MANSION," read a *New York Post* headline.

At first, Jackie did not want to interfere. Her press secretary, Nancy Tuckerman, released a statement saying that the Beales were living as they wished. But the discrepancy between Jackie's lifestyle and that of her aunt and cousin made it a sensational story. The bad publicity eventually forced Onassis to step in and pay to have the house repaired and maintained so the two women could remain living there.

Later, David and Albert Maysles, directors best known for the Rolling Stones documentary *Gimme Shelter*, directed an underground film entitled *Grey Gardens*. The film was initially conceived as a serious documentary about the gentrification of East Hampton, but somewhere along the way it was decided that the subject of the film would shift to focus almost entirely on the lifestyle of Edith and little Edie Beale. "They were so brilliantly, ingeniously, totally nuts—in the most fabulous way," says Peter Beard, who started the project. Everyone participating

in the film *Grey Gardens* had to wear flea collars around their ankles.

But part of the fascination with the film was clearly the Jackie connection. The two women spoke of her often and one of the cats was even named Ted Z. Kennedy. Wayne Koestenbaum, among others, has suggested that Edie represents Jackie's doppelganger, what she could have become if things had worked out just a little differently. In any event, the Maysles' film became a cult classic. Edith and little Edie became semi-celebrities and Edith even appeared briefly at a nightclub singing opera.

In February 1977 Edith died. Little Edie sold Grey Gardens to Ben Bradlee and Sally Quinn. Jackie was upset by the sale: she felt Bradlee had betrayed JFK with his favorable but less than hagiographic portrait of the president in *Conversations with Kennedy*. When the Bradlees first saw the house, it was still decrepit despite all the previous repairs. "The back wall of the house was flapping in the wind," recalls Quinn. The presence of so many cats caused Ben to have an immediate allergy attack and he ran from the house. Quinn went over to inspect the piano. "I plunked a couple of keys," she says, "and the piano collapsed." As Quinn surveyed the ruins, Edie did a little pirouette and proclaimed, "Isn't it divine? All it needs is a coat of paint."

flowers. She paid all her mother's medical bills and provided her with around-the-clock nursing assistance. Janet Auchincloss died in 1989.

Jackie remained enormously popular with the public, who had long since forgiven her for her marriage to Onassis. Simply by eating in a restaurant or quietly walking through a department store, she could upstage any Hollywood actress. In her forties and fifties, she still looked far younger than her years. She took superb care of herself, exercising regularly and never gaining weight. She would go for regular facials at Nardi salon in New York, and had a face-lift in the early 1980s. Her style now was more pared down—simple but elegant. In New York she could often be spotted strolling in pants and a Gap T-shirt or cashmere pullover. And, of course, there was her famous Jackie O. disguise—a scarf wrapped tightly around her face and dark sunglasses—which became an integral part of her wardrobe. Despite her attempts to camouflage herself, she was instantly recognizable—to almost everyone, that is. In 1984 she was introduced to author Isaac Bashevis Singer, and, assuming that the novelist would know who she was, told him, "I'm a writer, too." The aged novelist, completely unaware of her identity, replied, "That's very nice, girlie. Keep working and I'm sure you'll get somewhere."

Because the public remained fascinated with her, the press continued to cover Jackie's every move. The *Reader's Guide to Periodical Literature* has more listings for Jacqueline Lee Bouvier Kennedy than for any other living American woman. Much of the attention was unwanted; some of it was frightening. In 1981, prosecutors discovered that Mark David Chapman, the man convicted of assassinating John Lennon, had included Jackie on his hit list. Her nemesis, photographer Ron Galella, continued to take snapshots of Jackie, violating

Jackie with Maurice Templesman in Central Park, New York City.

his court injunction. He was forced to give her $10,000 and was prohibited from ever photographing her again.

Jackie's friends and family were under strict orders not to talk to the press. As John, Jr. once told a reporter who approached him for an interview, he couldn't cooperate because, he said, "My mother would kill me." Jackie never talked about her days in the White House. "Please let's not talk about the past," she would say to friends who questioned her. "I have to remain alive for myself. I don't want to dredge up the past." Yet occasionally Jackie provided glimpses of how she felt about her life. Once, Rosamond Bernier, wife of *New York Times* art critic John Russell, invited Jackie to a dinner party. One of the other guests that evening was English poet Stephen Spender. He asked Jackie what the one accomplishment was in her life of which she felt most proud. She thought about the question, then replied, "Well, I went through some pretty difficult times, and I kept my sanity."

But many of those around Jackie, both friends and casual observers, thought her greatest achievement was her children. Unlike their Kennedy cousins, many of whom were plagued with emotional and behavioral problems, both Caroline and John grew up to be well-adjusted. Caroline, who bore a striking resemblence to her father, is sensible and unpretentious. She dresses casually and one summer even took a lowly internship at the *New York Daily News.* A good student, Caroline attended Harvard as an undergraduate and then earned a law degree from Columbia, going on to practice law and coauthor two popular books about the Constitution. In July 1986, at age 28, Caroline married Ed Schlossberg, a forty-one-year-old conceptual artist. Jackie was pleased with her daughter's choice of a husband. At the reception, which took place on Cape Cod, Teddy toasted the mother of the bride, calling her "an extraordinary, gallant woman, Jack's only love." Caroline and Schlossberg had three children in Jackie's lifetime. Jackie loved being a grandmother and could often be spotted in Central Park with Caroline's children.

Tall and strikingly handsome, John, Jr. became a tabloid favorite (once named the sexiest man alive by *People*) who constantly had to battle the perception that he had better looks than brains, but which he reinforced by constantly biking and Rollerblading around Manhattan in shorts with no shirt. After graduating from Brown University, John dabbled a bit in acting before deciding, like his sister, to study law. Armed with a degree from New York University Law School, John took a job as an assistant prosecutor in the Manhattan district attorney's office and passed the bar on his third try. Unlike Caroline's relationships, John's romantic attachments generated tremendous amounts of press. Prior to his marriage in 1996 to Carolyn Bessette, John dated several actresses, including such starlets as Sarah Jessica Parker, Darryl Hannah, and Madonna—all apparently to his mother's chagrin. And like his father, John, Jr. did not seem to mind the press attention. Dissatisfied with his career as a prosecutor, in 1995 John launched his own magazine, *George*, a slick journal focusing on political personalities. Ironically, John had become a member of the press that his mother so despised.

According to biographer Ed Klein, who was a friend of Jackie's, the former First Lady worried constantly that her children were developing a negative impression of their father from all the revisionist histories of his life and presidency. Klein reports that Jackie would call up contemporaries of Jack's and invite them over with the express purpose of describing Jack's achievements and good qualities to the children.

Jackie had several relationships while in New York, including one with Pete Hamill, a handsome New York journalist. She eventually became involved in a long-term relationship that lasted over a dozen years with diamond merchant and financier Maurice Templesman. The match seemed unusual, at least at first. Templesman, who was a year younger than Jackie, was from an Orthodox Jewish background. He had originally met Jackie while she was First Lady. President Kennedy had often sought his advice on how to prepare for meetings with African leaders, and Templesman and his wife, Lily, were frequently invited to White House dinners. When he and Jackie became romantically involved, Templesman was still married to Lily. When Lily learned of the affair, she and her husband separated but did not divorce. Lily was strictly observant of Orthodox Jewish law and would not grant her husband a divorce, which meant he and Jackie could not marry.

Unlike Jackie's marriages, this relationship was conducted out of the glare of the spotlight. Unlike Onassis, Templesman was cultured and urbane. He disliked press scrutiny and never capitalized on his relationship with Jackie. They were discreet, but apparently also very romantic. "They hold hands in the theater, sit with their heads together at corner tables in restaurants, and kiss between courses," a friend said.

Templesman was Jackie's financial adviser, and by every indication, he advised her well, turning the $26 million she inherited from Onassis into well over $100 million. In 1978 she bought land on Martha's Vineyard for more than $1 million and, two years later, built a $3.6 million vacation house on it. Located in the remote section of the island called Gay Head, the nineteen-room estate (which she often referred to as her "little house") became Jackie's sanctuary.

For decades, American politicians had tried to associate themselves with the JFK legacy. In the summer of 1993, the newly elected Democratic president, Bill Clinton, vacationed on Martha's Vineyard. Jackie invited Clinton and his wife, Hillary, to her house and took the president and First Lady sailing aboard Templesman's yacht. Clinton had met JFK in the Rose Garden as a teenager and later tried to emulate him in his political career. Like his idol, Clinton knew the value of a photo op. The picture of Clinton, just forty-six, sailing with Jackie aboard a yacht evoked images of Camelot. The association was not an accident.

In October 1993 Jackie sat next to the Clintons at what

would be her last official public appearance: the rededication of the JFK Memorial Library. The following January she was diagnosed with non-Hodgkins lymphoma, cancer of the lymph nodes or glands. On February 10, Nancy Tuckerman made an announcement to the press about her condition. She explained that the cancer had been caught early and that Jackie had been undergoing chemotherapy. "There is an excellent prognosis," Tuckerman told the press. "You can never be absolutely sure, but the doctors are very, very optimistic." But on April 14, Jackie was hospitalized at Cornell Medical Center in New York. The cancer had spread; the doctors could not help her. After a week, Jackie chose to return to the comfort of her Fifth Avenue apartment. Throughout her illness, Templesman was at her bedside constantly. Jackie died on May 19, 1994, at age sixty-four.

Jackie with President Clinton and John, Jr. at the rededication of the JFK Library.

⟡ CAMELOT AT AUCTION ⟡

JACKIE'S JEWELRY BROUGHT
SOME OF THE HIGHEST PRICES
IN THE AUCTION.

Any doubts about Jackie's enduring place in the nation's consciousness were laid to rest when Sotheby's held her estate sale in April 1996.

More than five thousand items belonging to the former First Lady were auctioned off during a four-day period. A total of $34.5 million were raised over the course of the auction, $2.5 million alone from the sale of more than one hundred thousand copies of the glossy auction catalog. For the five days before the auction began, Sotheby's showroom was open, and nearly forty thousand people stood in line just for the opportunity to observe the merchandise. Although connoisseurs proclaimed most of the stuff worthless, auctiongoers spent outrageous amounts of money for the most mundane of Jackie objects.

What did they buy? An eclectic mix of items that ranged from an ordinary set of salt and pepper shakers, to Aaron Shikler's studies for his White House portraits of Jackie, to her 1992 metallic dark green BMW 325i. Serious, and seriously rich, collectors of JFK arcana drove up the price on such items as a set of the president's golf clubs, a cigar humidor given to him by comedian Milton Berle, and several of his many rocking chairs. The item of greatest historical significance was the summerhouse desk on which Kennedy had signed the Nuclear Test-Ban Treaty. The most expensive item was the forty-carat, marquise-shaped diamond engagement ring that Aristotle Onassis gave Jackie in 1968.

In a clever marketing strategy, Sotheby's placed low estimates on all the items in the auction catalog. Experienced auctiongoers realized the estimates were inaccurate, but it gave many the opportunity to dream about putting their own Jackie knickknack on the mantelpiece.

Some observers criticized John and Caroline for allowing the possessions of their very private mother to be rummaged through by the public and then sold to the highest bidder. *New York* magazine called it "viscerally cruel . . . for Caroline and John to auction off their mom as Home Shopping Network fodder." But Jackie herself is said to have suggested the sale. Nancy Tuckerman told *Time* in 1992 that "Jackie did mention in her will that the children, if they wanted to, should have an auction. It would be the practical thing to do." Perhaps, but there was something unseemly about Arnold Schwarzenegger, who married JFK's niece Maria Shriver, laying out $772,500 to buy golf clubs, a painting, and a desk set from members of his wife's own family.

If the children appeared less than dignified, those who spent outrageous amounts of money for what amounted to the "leftovers" of Jackie's estate looked even worse.

Only Jackie emerged, as always, unblemished.

A SAMPLE OF AUCTIONED ITEMS
- A GOLD AND BLACK ENAMEL LIGHTER INSCRIBED WITH A "J." ESTIMATED: $300–$400 SOLD FOR: $85,000
- A SILVER-CASED TIFFANY'S TAPE MEASURE WITH JACKIE'S INITIALS. ESTIMATED: $500–$700 SOLD FOR: $48,875
- CAROLINE'S ROCKING HORSE. ESTIMATED: $2,000 $3,000 SOLD FOR: $85,000
- A SMALL STOOL WITH A TORN, FADED, AND STAINED SATIN COVER. ESTIMATED: $100–$150 SOLD FOR: $33,350
- A SET OF McGREGOR WOODS, AND A BLACK AND RED MONOGRAMMED GOLF BAG. ESTIMATED: $700–$900 SOLD FOR: $772,500
- CIGAR HUMIDOR GIVEN TO JFK IN 1961 BY MILTON BERLE. ESTIMATED: $2,000–$2,500 SOLD FOR: $574,500
- A SET OF SILVER ASHTRAYS. ESTIMATED: $400–$600 SOLD FOR: $27,600
- THE DESK ON WHICH PRESIDENT JOHN F. KENNEDY SIGNED THE NUCLEAR TEST-BAN TREATY. ESTIMATED: $20,000–$30,000 SOLD FOR: $1,432,500
- FORTY-CARAT MARQUISE-SHAPED DIAMOND THAT WAS GIVEN AS AN ENGAGEMENT PRESENT BY ARISTOTLE ONASSIS. ESTIMATED: $500,000–$600,000 SOLD FOR: $2,587,500

Jackie's funeral, May 1994.

The next morning, John, Jr. came outside and read a statement to the press and the crowd that had assembled outside her
building to pay their last respects. "Last night at ten-fifteen,
my mother passed on. She was surrounded by her friends and
her family and the books and the people and the things that she
loved. And she did it her own way and on her own terms, and
we all feel lucky for that, and now she's in God's hands."

The private funeral sevice was held at St. Ignatius Loyola
Church, where Jackie had been baptized. Seven hundred people were in attendance. Many who weren't invited gathered
across the street, maintaining a respectful distance. Jackie
opted to be buried beside JFK at Arlington National Cemetery,

near the eternal flame that she herself had designed years before. In his eulogy Teddy Kennedy said, "I often think about what she said about Jack in December after he died. 'They made him a legend when he would have preferred to be a man.' Jackie would have preferred to be just herself, but the world insisted that she be a legend, too."

CHRONOLOGY

1929   July 28: Born in the Hamptons, Long Island,
        New York.
        December 22: Christened at St. Ignatius
        Loyola Church in New York.
1933   Sister, Caroline Lee, is born.
1936   September 30: Parents, Janet Lee and Jack Bouvier,
        separate for the first time.
1937   April: Parents reunite.
        September: Parents separate again.
1940   July 22: Parents divorce.
1942   Mother marries Hugh Auchincloss.
1944   Sent to Miss Porter's, a Connecticut boarding school.
1947   Summer: Comes out as a debutante.
        Autumn: Enrolls at Vassar College.
        Winter: Declared "Debutante of the Year."
1949   August: Goes to France for a year of study.
1950   Autumn: Transfers to George Washington University.
1951   Spring: Graduates from George Washington with a
            degree in French literature.
        Wins the *Vogue* Prix de Paris, but declines the prize.
        May: Meets John F. Kennedy, Jr.
        Autumn: Takes job as camera girl at the *Washington
        Times-Herald*.

1952	January 21: Announces engagement to John G. W. Husted, Jr.
	April: Breaks off engagement to Husted and begins to date Kennedy.
	July 4: JFK introduces her to his family.
1953	June 24: Announces engagement to JFK.
	September 12: Weds JFK at St. Mary's Roman Catholic Church in Newport, Rhode Island
1955	July: Miscarries first pregnancy.
1956	August 23: Gives birth to stillborn child.
1957	August: Father, Black Jack Bouvier, dies.
	November 27: Daughter, Caroline, born.
1960	November: JFK defeats Richard M. Nixon to become thirty-fifth president of the United States.
	November 26: Son, John, Jr., born.
1961	January 20: JFK takes the oath of office.
	First trips to Paris and Vienna as First Lady.
1963	August 9: Newborn son, Patrick, dies.
	November 22: JFK assassinated in Dallas, Texas.
	November 25: JFK buried in Arlington National Cemetary.
1968	October 20: Marries Aristotle Onassis.
1973	January 22: Stepson Alexander dies in plane crash.
1974	March 15: Aristotle Onassis dies.
1975	September: Hired as assistant editor at Viking Press.
1977	Resigns from Viking.
	Becomes an associate editor at Doubleday.
1982	Promoted to editor at Doubleday.
1986	July: Daughter Caroline marries Ed Schlossberg.
1994	May 19: Dies of non-Hodgkins lymphoma.

BIBLIOGRAPHY

BOOKS

Adler, Bill, editor. *The Uncommon Wisdom of Jacqueline Kennedy Onassis: A Portrait in Her Own Words*. New York: Citadel Press, 1994.

Anderson, Christopher. *Jack and Jackie: Portrait of an American Marriage*. New York: William Morrow, 1996.

Anthony, Carl Sferrazza. *First Ladies, Volume II: The Saga of the Presidents' Wives and Their Power, 1960–1990*. New York: William Morrow, 1991.

Birmingham, Stephen. *Jacqueline Bouvier Kennedy Onassis*. New York: Grosset & Dunlap, 1978.

Black, Allida M. *Casting Her Own Shadow: Eleanor Roosevelt and the Shaping of Post-War Liberalism*. New York: Columbia University Press, 1996.

Boller, Jr., Paul F. *Presidential Wives*. New York: Oxford University Press, 1988.

Bradlee, Ben. *Conversations with Kennedy*. New York: W. W. Norton, 1975.

———*A Good Life: Newspapering and Other Adventures*. New York: Simon and Schuster, 1995.

Cassini, Oleg. *A Thousand Days of Magic: Dressing Jacqueline Kennedy for the White House*. New York: Rizzoli, 1995.

Collier, Peter, and David Horowitz. *The Kennedys: An American Drama*. New York: Summit Books, 1984.

David, Lester. *Jacqueline Kennedy Onassis: A Portrait of Her Private Years*. New York: Birch Lane Press, 1994.

Davis, John H. *The Bouviers: Portrait of an American Family*. New York: Farrar, Straus and Giroux, 1969.

————*The Kennedys: Dynasty and Disaster 1848–1983*. New York: McGraw-Hill, 1984.

Davis, L. J. *Onassis: Aristotle and Christina*. New York: St. Martin's Press, 1986.

Heymann, C. David. *A Woman Named Jackie: An Intimate Biography of Jacqueline Bouvier Kennedy Onassis*. New York: Lyle Stuart, 1989.

Kelley, Kitty. *Jackie Oh!* Secaucus, NJ: Lyle Stuart, 1978.

Kennedy, John F. *Profiles in Courage*. New York: Harper & Brothers, 1955.

Klein, Edward. *All Too Human*. New York: Simon and Schuster, 1996.

Koestenbaum, Wayne. *Jackie Under My Skin: Interpreting an Icon*. New York: Farrar, Straus, and Giroux, 1995.

Lash, Joseph P. *Eleanor and Franklin*. New York: Smithmark, 1995.

Leamer, Laurence. *The Kennedy Women*. New York: Villard, 1994.

Manchester, William. *The Death of a President—1963*. New York: Harper & Row, 1967.

Martin, Ralph G. *A Hero for Our Time*. New York: Macmillan, 1983.

Matthews, Christopher. *Kennedy and Nixon*. New York: Simon and Schuster, 1996.

Paglia, Camille. *Vamps and Tramps*. New York: Vintage, 1994.

Reeves, Thomas, *A Question of Character*. Rocklin, CA: Prima, 1992.

Salinger, Pierre. *With Kennedy*. New York: Doubleday, 1966.

Schlesinger, Jr., Arthur M. *Robert Kennedy and His Times*. New York: Ballantine, 1978.

Suarés, J. C., and Spencer J. Beck. *Uncommon Grace: Reminiscences and Photographs of Jacqueline Bouvier Kennedy Onassis*. Charlottesville, VA: Thomasson-Grant, 1994.

Tapert, Annette, and Diana Edkins. *The Power of Style: The Women Who Defined the Art of Living Well.* New York: Crown, 1994.

Thayer, Mary Van Rensselaer. *Jacqueline Bouvier Kennedy.* New York: Doubleday, 1961.

Truman, Margaret. *First Ladies: An Intimate Group Portrait of White House Wives.* New York: Random House, 1995.

Tuckerman, Nancy. Preface to *The Estate of Jacqueline Kennedy Onassis.* New York: Sotheby's, 1996.

Vidal, Gore. *Palimpsest: A Memoir.* New York: Random House, 1995.

West, J. B., with Mary Lynn Kotz. *Upstairs at the White House: My Life with the First Ladies.* New York: Coward, McCann and Geoghegan, 1973.

White, Theodore H. *The Making of the President, 1960: A Narrative History of American Politics in Action.* New York: Atheneum, 1961.

———*In Search of History: A Personal Adventure.* New York: Warner Books, 1978.

PERIODICALS

Look

New York

New York Daily News

New York Times

Time

Vogue

Washingtonian

Washington Post

SOURCES

CHAPTER ONE
RESOURCES

Birmingham; Davis; Heymann; Klein; Lash; Thayer; Tuckerman; Vidal.

INTERVIEWS

Jamie Auchincloss, Evan Thomas

SOURCES

p. 4 *"The seed had gone to"*: Author interview with Auchincloss.

p. 7 *"She [Jackie] was of tougher"*: ibid.

p. 8 *"They didn't know what"*: Thayer, p. 27.

p. 8 *"There was a picture"*: Author interview with Auchincloss.

p. 8 *"Jackie was acting up"*: ibid.

p. 8 *"I know you love"*: Thayer, p. 20.

p. 9 *"Before he passed out"*: Klein, p. 34.

p. 9 For one account of Eleanor Roosevelt's relationship with her father, see Lash.

p. 12 *"SOCIETY BROKER SUED FOR DIVORCE"*: Quoted in Heymann, p. 40.

p. 12 *"The word 'swashbuckling' "*: Author interview with Auchincloss.

p. 13 *"the second generation"*: Davis, p. 210.

p. 13 *"It was a very"*: Author interview with Auchincloss.

p. 13 *"had changed his name"*: Vidal, p. 72.

p. 13 *"That was one of the"*: Author interview with Auchincloss.

p. 16 *"I just know no one"*: Birmingham, p. 79.

p. 17 *"That one, Daddy?"*: Klein, p. 37.

p. 17 *"wearing a stolen blanket"*: Heymann, p. 58.

p. 19 Jackie's full entry in the yearbook: Birmingham, p. 163.

CHAPTER TWO

RESOURCES

Adler; Anderson; Conconi; Heymann; Klein; Thayer; *Vogue; Washingtonian.*

INTERVIEW

Jamie Auchincloss

SOURCES

p. 21 *"To meet Miss Jacqueline Lee Bouvier"*: Thayer, p. 68.

p. 21 *"Many women of Newport"*: Author interview with Auchincloss.

p. 22 *"a lovely white tulle gown"*: Thayer, p. 72.

p. 22 *"siren suit"*: Heymann, p. 62.

p. 23 *"America is a country of "*: Quoted in Thayer, p. 73.

p. 24 *"I usually tried to choose"*: Heymann, p. 63.

p. 26 *"Jackie was never sexually"*: Heymann, p. 68.

p. 29 *"Gets hysterical and thinks I'm"*: Adler, p. 8.

p. 30 *"I loved it [Paris] more than"*: From a reprint of Jackie's essay that appeared in *Vogue,* August 1994.

p. 31 *"As to physical"* and ensuing: ibid.

p. 32 *"Mark my words,"*: Klein, p. 74.

p. 33 *"Marry someone who will constantly"*: Conconi, p. 108.

p. 34 *"A vodka martini"*: Quoted in "Girl Reporter," Conconi, *The Washingtonian,* July 1994, p. 42.

p. 34 *"Just once before"*: Klein, p. 107.

p. 35 *"He's always away"* and ensuing questions: All questions were originally published in the *Washington Times-Herald,* and have since been reported in many sources.

p. 35 *"Her questions"*: Koestenbaum, p. 184.

p. 35 *"Her looks were"*: Heymann, p. 92.

p. 35 *"She worked hard"*: Conconi, p. 43.

p. 36 *"Are you still hiring"* and ensuing: Thayer, p. 83.

CHAPTER THREE

RESOURCES

Adler; Anderson; Collier and Horowitz; Davis: *The Kennedys;*
  Heymann; Kelley; Klein; Leamer; Martin; Reeves.

INTERVIEW

Jamie Auchincloss

SOURCES

p. 40 *"weigh more and have"*: Anderson, p. 91.

p. 40 *"They hardly spoke"*: Heymann, p. 89.

p. 40 *"What no one seemed"*: Klein, p. 113.

p. 42 *"Don't listen to any of the drivel"*: Heymann, p. 105.

p. 42 *"You're one of the nicest"*: Klein, p. 117.

p. 43 *"Goes to a hairdresser"* and ensuing: Davis, pp. 150–151.

p. 44 *"Icebergs"* and *"submerged"*: ibid.

p. 44 *"What I want more"*: Collier and Horowitz, p. 197.

p. 44 *"How can I explain these"*: Leamer, p. 431.

p. 45 *"Jac-Lean"*: Collier and Horowitz, p. 193.

p. 46 *"They would fall over"*: ibid.

p. 46 *"They'll kill me before"*: Reeves, p. 113.

p. 46 *"It's enough for me"*: Heymann, p. 113.

p. 47 *"It's not what you are"*: Anderson, p. 107.

p. 47 *"A politician has to have"*: Heymann, p. 115.

p. 47 *"Talked about sports, politics"*: Kelley, p. 12.

p. 50 *"ARTICLES EXCELLENT, BUT"*: Martin, p. 80.

p. 50 *"How can you live with"*: Leamer, p. 433.

p. 50 *"Twenty-four hours"* and ensuing: Klein, p. 149.

p. 51 *"Hopeful debutantes"*: *New York Daily News,* June 23, 1953.

p. 52 *"Too much"* and ensuing: Heymann, p. 122.

p. 53 *"Newport had filed"*: Klein, p. 169.

p. 53 *"an atrocious mass"*: Heymann, p. 127.

p. 54 *"Far surpassed"*: *New York Times,* September 13, 1953.

p. 54 *"I'll never know"* and ensuing: Author interview with Auchincloss.

p. 54 *"Aside from the"* and ensuing: Anderson, p. 6.

CHAPTER FOUR

RESOURCES

Anderson; Black; Bradlee: *Conversations with Kennedy;* Collier and Horowitz; Heymann; Kelley, Kennedy; Koestenbaum; Lawliss; Leamer; Martin; Matthews; Reeves; *Washington Post.*

INTERVIEWS

Charlie Peters, Evan Thomas

SOURCES

p. 59 *"I'm an old-fashioned wife"*: Martin, p. 92.

p. 60 *"After the first year"*: Collier and Horowitz, p. 197.

p. 60 *"Curious inquiring mind"*: Anderson, p. 131.

p. 60 *"[Jack] was so sick"*: ibid, p. 140.

p. 62 *"I don't think there is"*: Matthews, p. 101.

p. 62 *"It was the first"*: Martin, p. 96

p. 62 *"He had a hole"*: ibid, p. 97.

p. 63 *"This book would not"*: Kennedy, p.

p. 63 *"If Jack didn't write"*: Heymann, p. 175.

p. 63 *"I think Jack supervised"*: Klein, p. 193.

p. 65 *"Maybe he thought"*: Collier and Horowitz, p. 196.

p. 66 *"someone who understands"*: Black, p. 178.

p. 67 *"You're pretty much in love"* and ensuing: Anderson, p. 166.

p. 68 *"SENATOR KENNEDY ON"*: *Washington Post,* August 25, 1956.

p. 68 *"baby-making machine"*: Heymann, p. 350.

p. 70 *"had a little too much"*: Kelley, p. 45.

p. 70 *"I thought she would"*: Author interview with Peters.

p. 70 *"I have a solution"*: Anderson, p. 115.

p. 70 *"Acapulco"*: Martin, p. 100.

p. 70 *"I think it's so unfair"*: Anderson, p. 222.

p. 71 *"I couldn't possibly"* and ensuing: Reeves, p. 205.

p. 71 *"Just keep on with"*: Martin, p. 151.

p. 71 *"Goodbye"* and ensuing: Leamer, p. 493.

p. 71 *"to pull some invisible"*: Bradlee, p. 29.

p. 71 *"in the 'At Home with the Kennedys'"*: Koestenbaum, p. 182.

p. 72 *"Dammit, Jackie, why is it that"*: Reeves, p. 145.

p. 74 *"I suppose I won't be able to"*: Kelley, p. 91.

p. 75 *"When's Inauguration Day?"*: Martin, p. 227.

CHAPTER FIVE

RESOURCES

Adler; Anderson; Anthony; Boller; Bradlee: *Conversations with Kennedy;* Cassini; Kelley; Klein; Koestenbaum; Manchester; Tapert and Edkins; Truman; Vidal; West; *Look.*

INTERVIEWS

Jamie Auchincloss, Ben Bradlee

SOURCES

p. 77 *"It was so crowded that"* and ensuing: Kelley, p. 103.

p. 78 *"Oh, for God's sake, Jackie"*: Anderson, p. 233.

p. 80 *"I talked to her like a"*: Cassini, p. 30.

p. 80 *"Make sure no one has"*: ibid.

p. 80 *"I refuse to have Jack's"*: ibid.

p. 80 *"Protect me—as I seem"*: ibid.

p. 80 *"There may just be a few"*: ibid.

p. 81 *"hotel that had been decorated"*: Heymann, p. 254.

p. 82 *"We're nothing but sitting ducks"*: Anderson, p. 239.

p. 84 *"You were wonderful"*: Martin, p. 12.

p. 84 *"There was so much I wanted"*: Anderson, p. 249.

p. 84 *"I don't know a better way to spend"*: Kelley, p. 119.

p. 84 *"Just a bunch of people standing"*: ibid., p. 120.

p. 85 *"My mother just chatted"*: Author interview with Jamie Auchincloss.

p. 85 *"She didn't realize that my mother"*: ibid.

p. 86 *"My parents were supposed to be"*: ibid.

p. 86 *"I sat next to Eleanor Roosevelt"*: ibid.

p. 86 *"Jackie was playing completely dumb"*: ibid.

p. 87 *"I would practically break"*: Anthony, p. 55.

p. 88 *"Confirming Albert Breeson"*: ibid., p. 54.

p. 88 *"I mean kings and queens"*: Klein, p. 278.

p. 88 *"Can't we give them"*: ibid.

p. 88 *"If you bungle raising"*: Anthony, p. 46.

p. 88 *"If I were to add political duties"*: Martin, p. 520.

p. 89 *"Mrs. Kennedy dropped everything"*: West, p. 204.

p. 89 *"No Mamie pink on the walls"*: Adler, p. 49.

p. 89 *"Would be sacrilege merely to"*: Anderson, p. 244.

p. 91 *"In this job, there's always"*: Anthony, p. 47.

p. 91 *"It was the first time"* and ensuing: Anderson, p. 273.

p. 91 *"She walked through the"*: Quoted in Kelley, p. 149.

p. 91 *"like a docent on drugs"*: Koestenbaum, p. 44.

p. 94 *"shared the conviction"*: Anthony, p. 37.

p. 94 *"What a joy that literacy is"*: ibid.

p. 94 *"It's the Jackie Kennelrock Look!"*: ibid., p. 77.

p. 95 *"Or better yet, as a president's wife."*: ibid., p. 47.

p. 95 *"Reporters"*: Anderson, p. 284.

p. 95 *"You have to remember"*: Author interview with Ben Bradlee.

p. 95 *"It got to be a game"*: Anderson, p. 277.

p. 95 *"I don't give a damn"*: ibid., p. 278.

p. 96 *"I'm sorry, Jackie, but when"*: ibid., p. 283.

p. 96 *"Mrs. Kennedy's charm"*: Anthony, p. 41.

p. 96 *"I now have more confidence"*: ibid., p. 42.

p. 96 *"I do not think it's altogether"*: Boller, p. 364.

p. 97 *"The worst thing in my life"*: Klein, p. 290.

p. 97 *"Oh, Mr. Chairman, don't bore me"*: Anthony, p. 43.

p. 97 *"Posed next to grandmotherly"* and ensuing: Koestenbaum, p. 153.

p. 98 *"Jacqueline Kennedy had"* : *Time*, August 31, 1962.

p. 98 *"A LITTLE MORE CAROLINE"*: Klein, p. 316.

p. 99 *"She used to leave funny"*: Anderson, p. 266.

p. 99 *"If it was earlier in"*: Klein, p. 321.

p. 100 *"Republican version of"*: *Look*, October 31, 1967.

p. 101 *"she knows how to do"*: Anthony, p. 319.

p. 101 *"I wonder if her interest"*: Vidal, p. 326.

p. 103 *"There's only one thing"*: Manchester, p. 8.

p. 103 *"The most affectionate embrace"*: Bradlee, p. 206.

p. 104 *"I could not accept his"*: Kelley, p. 211.

CHAPTER SIX

RESOURCES

Anderson; Birmingham; Collier and Horowitz; Editors of *Life;* Heymann; Kelley; *Look;* Manchester; Salinger; Schlesinger; Truman; White.

SOURCES

p. 107 *"BIENVENIDO, MR. AND MRS. PRESIDENT"*and ensuing: Manchester, p. 75. Manchester remains the primary source for any discussion of John F. Kennedy's assassination.

p. 107 *"Mr. President, your crowd here"*: ibid., p. 80.

p. 108 *"Where's Jackie?"*: ibid., p. 114.

p. 108 *"Two years ago I introduced"*: ibid., p. 120.

p. 108 *"We're heading into"*: ibid, p. 121.

p. 109 *"You sure can't say"*: ibid, p. 153.

p. 109 *"My God, what are they"*: ibid, p. 160.

p. 109 *"God, they are going to"*: ibid., p. 157.

p. 109 *"Jack, Jack, can you"*: Anderson, p. 365.

p. 109 *"You know he's dead"* and ensuing: Quoted in Anderson, p. 365.

p. 110 *"I only wish things could"*: Heymann, p. 428.

p. 111 *"Sweetheart, listen"*: ibid.

p. 111 *"Colonel Cornpone"*: Martin, p. 9.

p. 111 *"Good God, do I have"*: Klein, p. 292.

p. 112 *"Mrs. Kennedy, your husband has"*: Manchester, p. 188.

p. 112 *"Let them see what"*: Kelley, p. 231.

p. 113 *"Silly little"*: Heymann, p. 420.

p. 113 *"I can't help crying, Caroline"*: Manchester, p. 409.

p. 116 *"We're going to say goodbye"*: Kelley, p. 241.

p. 117 *"Don't be frightened of this"*: Truman, p. 170.

p. 119 *"pink-rose ridges"* and ensuing: White, p. 522.

p. 119 *"make certain that Jack"*: ibid, p. 524.

p. 119 *"a misreading"* and ensuing: *Newsweek*, May 30, 1994.

p. 120 *"He is really very shy"*: Kelley, p. 260.

p. 120 *"You knew that if"*: Leamer, p. 443.

p. 120 *"Staff members saw the"*: ibid., p. 608.

p. 121 *"Can anyone understand how it"*: Kelley, p. 250.

p. 121 *"The knowledge of the affection"*: Editors of *Life*.

p. 122 *"Now I think I should"*: *Look*, November 17, 1964, p. 36.

p. 123 *"Taking you anyplace is like"*: Heymann, p. 465.

p. 123 *"Do you know what I"*: Schlesinger, p. 921.

p. 124 *"She is a totally misunderstood"*: Birmingham, p. 228.

p. 125 *"I hate this country"* and ensuing: Collier and Horowitz, p. 367.

CHAPTER SEVEN

RESOURCES

Birmingham; Bradlee: *A Good Life;* Collier and Horowitz; Davis: *Onassis;* Heymann; Kelley; Klein; Koestenbaum; Martin; Matthews; Truman.

SOURCES

p. 129 *"Americans can't understand"* and ensuing: Kelley, p. 322.

p. 129 *"The widow"* and ensuing: Heymann, p. 511.

p. 129 *"Jackie did well to give"*: ibid., p. 514.

p. 131 *"Mrs. Hugh D. Auchincloss has asked me"*: Kelley, p. 307.

p. 131 *"I did not expect a dowry"*: Heymann, p. 504.

p. 131 *"We wish our wedding to be"*: Birmingham, p. 198.

p. 132 *"HOW COULD YOU?"*: Truman, p. 346.

p. 132 *"JACKIE WEDS BLANK CHECK"*: Heymann, p. 513.

p. 132 *"The reaction here is anger"*: Leamer, p. 643.

p. 133 *"I consider that my life"*: Bradlee, p. 262.

p. 133 *"That's better than freezing"*: Martin, p. 573.

p. 134 *"Jackie is like a little bird"* and ensuing: Birmingham, p. 187.

p. 136 *"grievous mental anguish"*: Heymann, p. 535.

p. 138 *"Lee was always the pretty"*: Collier and Horowitz, p. 192.

p. 138 *"Pathetic, lamentable"*: Heymann, p. 483.

p. 138 *"Lee was the only woman"*: Kelley, p. 195.

p. 139 *"I always lived in"*: Matthews, p. 293.

p. 140 *"To Christina it seemed as though Jackie"*: Heymann, p. 576.

p. 141 *"She wants my money"*: ibid., p. 579.

p. 141 *"We will not dignify those charges"*: ibid., p. 580.

p. 142 *"Aristotle Onassis rescued me"* and ensuing: Birmingham, p. 198.

p. 143 *"What amazes me "*: Koestenbaum, p. 257.

p. 143 *"Throughout the world"*: Heymann, p. 584.

p. 143 *"Miss Christina Onassis is very much distressed"*: Davis, pp. 208–209.

CHAPTER EIGHT

RESOURCES

Birmingham; David; Heymann; Klein; *New York;* Suarés and Beck; *Time.*

INTERVIEW

Sally Quinn

SOURCES

p. 146 *"I recognized what a boon she could be"*: Heymann, p. 591.

p. 146 *"She didn't know a lot about"*: ibid., p. 593.

p. 147 *"Anybody associated"*: David, p. 193.

p. 148 *"What has been sad for many women"*: ibid., p. 205.

p. 149 *"Kennedy men are like that"*: Heymann, p. 606.

p. 149 *"Joan, do you really expect life to be"*: ibid., p. 643.

p. 151 *"JACKIE'S AUNT TOLD"*: New York Post, January 10, 1972.

p. 151 *"They were so brilliantly"*: Heymann, p. 569.

p. 151 *"The back wall"* and ensuing: Author interview with Sally Quinn.

p. 152 *"I'm a writer, too"*: ibid, pp. 634–635.

p. 153 *"My mother would kill me"*: David, p. 7.

p. 153 *"Please let's not talk about"*: Klein, p. 356.

p. 154 *"Well, I went through"*: Heymann, p. 598.

p. 154 *"An extraordinary, gallant woman"*: ibid., p. 642.

p. 156 *"They hold hands in the theater"*: David, p. 179.

p. 157 *"There is an excellent prognosis"*: ibid., p. xvi.

p. 159 *"viscerally cruel"*: *New York,* April 29, 1996.

p. 159 *"Jackie did mention"*: *Time,* May 6, 1994.

p. 160 *"Last night at ten-fifteen, my mother"*: Suarés and Beck, p. 102.

p. 160 *"I often think about what she"*: David, p. 243.

PHOTOGRAPHY CREDITS

pp. iv, 70 © Cornell Capa/Magnum Photos, Inc.

pp. 1, 77, 100 courtesy of John F. Kennedy Library

p. 2 © Molly Thayer Collection/Magnum Photos, Inc.

pp. 3, 9 courtesy of Photofest

p. 6 © Molly Thayer Collection/Magnum Photos, Inc.

p. 15 © Molly Thayer Collection/Magnum Photos, Inc.

p. 18 © Molly Thayer Collection/Magnum Photos, Inc.

p. 20 © Robert Meservey/Magnum Photos, Inc.

pp. 21, 28 courtesy of Photofest

p. 23 © Robert Meservey/Magnum Photos, Inc.

p. 34 courtesy of Photofest

p. 38 courtesy of Photofest

pp. 39, 45 courtesy of Archive Photos

p. 48 courtesy of Dalmas/SIPA Press

p. 53 courtesy of Hulton Deutsch/SIPA Press

p. 56 © Eve Arnold/Magnum Photos, Inc.

pp. 57, 58 © HY Peskin/FPG International

p. 74 courtesy of FPG International

p. 76 courtesy of AP/Wide World Photos

p. 85 courtesy of John F. Kennedy Library

p. 93 courtesy of Photofest

p. 106 © Elliott Erwitt/Magnum Photos, Inc.

pp. 107, 120 courtesy of Photofest

p. 110 courtesy of John F. Kennedy Library

p. 115 courtesy of John F. Kennedy Library

p. 124 courtesy of Archive Photos/Popperphoto

p. 126 courtesy of Archive Photos

pp. 127, 142 courtesy of SIPA Press

p. 134 courtesy of Photofest

p. 144 courtesy of Archive Photos

pp. 145, 157 courtesy of AP/Wide World Photos

p. 150 courtesy of Photofest

p. 153 courtesy of Marcel Thomas/SIPA Press

p. 158 courtesy of AP/Wide World Photos

p. 160 courtesy of AP/Wide World Photos

INDEX

Canfield, Michael   47, 138

Casals, Pablo   92–93

Cassini, Igor   23–24

Cassini, Oleg   79–80

Chapman, Mark David   152

Churchill, Sir Winston   64

Clifford, Clark   63, 90

Clinton, Bill   156–157

Clinton, Hillary   101, 156

clothing   16, 22, 53, 79–80,
    83, 132
    "Jackie Look"   79–80, 94,
        152

Collingwood, Charles   91

Connally, John   109

Cushing, Richard Cardinal
    52, 83, 129

de Gaulle, Charles   30, 96, 116

De Pauw, Linda Grant
    146–147

De Renty, Countess Guyot and
    family   28–29

Doubleday (publishers)   147

drama, interest in   16

Duke, Doris   4

Eisenhower, Mamie   78, 81, 89

engagements   37, 39–40, 42,
    47, 51

Equal Rights Amendment   148

Europe   27–30, 33, 64

first lady
    cultural agenda as   92–94

family agenda as   87
    popularity as   94–96, 97

France, experiences in
    27–29, 96

Gabor, Zsa Zsa   50–51

Galella, Ron   136, 152

genealogy   13, 78

George Washington University
    30–32

Grey Gardens (East Hampton,
    NY)   150–151

Grier, Rosie   148

Guinzburg, Thomas   146–147

Hamill, Pete   155

Hammersmith Farm (Newport,
    RI)   14, 21, 52, 67, 103,
    149

Hamptons (NY)   5, 6, 7,
    150–151

Hepburn, Audrey   30

housewife, role as   19, 59–60,
    87

humor, sense of   16, 17, 70,
    87, 99

Huntley, Chet   66–67

Husted, John G. W., Jr.   37,
    39–40, 42–43

Jackson, Michael   147

Johnson, Lady Bird   110–111,
    112, 117

Johnson, Lyndon   73,
    110–111, 112

Onassis, Alexander   129–130,
   137, 139–140
Onassis, Aristotle   64,
   103–104, 113, 124–125,
   127–131, 140, 141
   marriage to   130–132
Onassis, Christina   129–130,
   135, 137, 140, 142–143
Plimpton, George   30, 123
politics   26–27, 41, 47,
   51–52, 59, 64, 70–71,
   72–75, 77, 87–88, 104, 148
Powers, Dave   42, 62, 107
pregnancies   65–67, 72, 77,
   78–79, 102
press
   member of   33–36, 41, 44,
      50
   object of   6, 23–24, 51,
      67–68, 82, 91, 94–95,
      118–119, 122–123, 132,
      136–137, 141–142, 143,
      153
Quinn, Sally   151
Radziwill, Lee   *see* Bouvier,
   Caroline Lee
Radziwill, Stanislas (Stas)   98,
   138
Reagan, Nancy   100–101
religion   70, 129
reserve, in character   10, 11,
   24, 25, 44, 71, 84

romance, experience of   26,
   30, 37, 155–156
Roosevelt, Eleanor   10, 100
Salinger, Pierre   77, 79, 90
Schlossberg, Ed   154
schooling   8–9, 16–18, 24–32
Schwarzenegger, Arnold   159
Shaw, Maude   71, 72, 79, 113
Sinatra, Frank   82, 101
Singer, Isaac Bashevis   152
Skorpios, Greece   131, 132,
   133, 137
Smathers, George   63, 68
society   12, 16, 21–24
   Auchinclosses and   14
   Bouviers and Lees and   3–4
   Kennedys and   46
Sorensen, Ted   63
Steinem, Gloria   146, 147
Stevenson, Adlai   65, 104
style   24, 30, 70–71, 78–79,
   94–95, 132, 152
Templesman, Maurice
   155–156, 157
Thayer, Mary Van Rensselaer
   78, 85
Tuckerman, Nancy   16, 19,
   54, 131, 141, 147, 151, 157
Turnure, Pamela   77–78
Vassar College (Poughkeepsie,
   NY)   24–26, 27, 30
Vidal, Gore   13, 14, 101

ACKNOWLEDGMENTS

I'm deeply indebted to Kate Fillion, Jay Carney, Mickey Kaus, and Christopher Hitchens, who read and edited large portions of the book.

Thanks also to my editor, Tom Dyja, my agent, Arthur Kaminsky, and his assistant, Ana Rodriguez.

In addition, the following people offered valuable assistance and support: Eli Attie, Ralph Alswang, Jamie Auchincloss, Antony Blinken, Laura Blumenfeld, Michael Cantor, Daniel Cass, Matt Cooper, John Duffy, Joann Elgart, Bruce Feiler, Jonathan Foreman, Angie Hunt, Wayne Koestenbaum, Karen Lehrman, Maura Moynihan, Dawn Perlmutter, Mrs. Howard C. Peterson, Jr., John Podhoretz, Esther Singer, Jenny Springer, Evan Thomas, Bob Weinstein. Finally, I'm especially grateful to my family for their constant love and encouragement. Special thanks to my mother, Susan Garfin, who read early drafts of several chapters.

ABOUT THE AUTHOR

Ellen Ladowsky writes about style and the political scene on Capitol Hill in Washington, D.C., for major publications, including the *New Yorker*, the *New Republic*, the *Washington Post*, *Mirabella*, the *New York Times*, *Newsweek*, and the *Wall Street Journal*.